FIELDS OF GREEN

Fields of Green

THE CELTIC DREAM TEAM

RODDY FORSYTH

MAINSTREAM
PUBLISHING

EDINBURGH AND LONDON

Photo credits
The author and publishers are grateful to *Celtic View* for permission to reproduce the photographs in this book.

This edition 1997

First published in Great Britain in 1996 by
MAINSTREAM PUBLISHING COMPANY (EDINBURGH) LTD
7 Albany Street
Edinburgh EH1 3UG

ISBN 1 84018 015 3 (paper)
ISBN 1 85158 888 4 (cased)

A catalogue record for this book is available from the British Library

Printed and bound in Great Britain by Butler and Tanner Ltd, Frome

Contents

Introduction

AN invitation to compile an account of Celtic's most memorable games seems at first sight to amount to a smallish job like, say, editing the *Encyclopaedia Britannica*. In order to keep the project within bounds and allow the reader to have a chance of finishing the book before the end of the century, it was decided to confine the number of contributors to a compact dozen — one manager and 11 players over the past 30 years.

Billy McNeill was the obvious choice of manager because he alone has occupied the position twice. The selection of players was bound to be more contentious and so it should be. Every supporter has his favourites. Some will ask, where are Jimmy Johnstone, Tommy Gemmell, Bertie Auld, Kenny Dalglish, Frank McAvennie? The list of options cannot be short and that reflects Celtic's stature over many years as a Scottish institution and a European football power. We did not set out to compile an all-time Celtic greats' XI, but rather to tell the tale of dramatic passages in the club's history through the eyes of those who took part.

It was decided to exclude the European Cup final because so many exhaustive accounts of that occasion have already found their way into print. The players represent every department of the team, from goalkeeper, through defence, midfield and wing to centre forward.

Every contributor has one crucial characteristic in common. It can be said without fear of contradiction that their commitment to Celtic has been absolute. Each man cites the club as his greatest love in football. Their accounts recall games which have become part of the mythology of Celtic, by turns dramatic, comic, painful and inspiring . . . but always enthralling. Their tales will entertain those who know the history as well as those who may open these pages curious to discover what makes the Celtic legend so enduring and extraordinary. It has been a privilege to be able to write about them. I hope you find them a pleasure to read.

R.F. 1996

Charlie Nicholas

RANGERS 0 CELTIC 1

18 April 1981

IF complimentary nicknames are a measure of affection, Charlie Nicholas must have a claim to be the best loved player ever to have worn the hoops. In Paul Lunney's encyclopaedic *Celtic: A Complete Record* the list under Nicholas's entry includes 'Darlin' Charlie', 'the Cannonball Kid', 'Bonnie Prince Charlie', 'Champagne Charlie' and 'Slick Nick'. To his team-mates he has always been 'Charlie Nick' and the book might also have included 'Cheekie Charlie', a description which resurfaced conveniently for the headline writers as late as February 1996, four months before he quit playing, when Nicholas was the star performer for Clyde against Rangers in a Scottish Cup-tie at Broadwood – the Bully Wee led the Ibrox millionaires 1–0 with more than an hour played – and he casually knocked the ball through Paul Gascoigne's legs in full view of a nationwide viewing audience on satellite television.

Gascoigne sportingly congratulated Nicholas on the nutmeg, a case of one singularly gifted footballer saluting the talent of another. For Nicholas it was a late flourish in a career which had rarely failed to offer entertainment on and off the park since he played his first full game for Celtic on 14 August 1979, a Glasgow Cup-tie against Queen's Park at Hampden, where the 17-year-old scored in a 3–1 win.

He was a conjurer, a trickster, a prodigy who refused to be overawed – above all, a resolutely individual player. Yet the match Nicholas values above all others may surprise many Celtic supporters and so too might his reason for choosing it. The game in question took place at Ibrox on 18 April 1981, an afternoon when a 1–0 victory over Rangers confirmed another Celtic title win, although they were not technically acknowledged as champions until their next fixture because Aberdeen, with a hugely inferior goal difference, could theoretically overtake them.

Nicholas was the scorer of the single goal which settled the issue, but although he relishes the memory of such a decisive strike, that is not why he savours this game. Nor is it because the critics were impressed by what they saw. Alan Davidson, whose report appeared in the Saturday Pink edition of the *Evening Times*, began by writing: 'An undistinguished Old Firm match seldom came close to the predictions.'

It is because, as Charlie himself eloquently says: 'It was simply the best team performance I ever took part in at any stage of my career. Nothing can compare with the thrill of running out for the first time at Celtic Park, which I would say must be the single most enjoyable moment I ever experienced in football. But that afternoon at Ibrox was definitely the most satisfying performance I can look back on.'

Given Charlie's penchant for fuelling the gossip columns in his younger days – hence the cascade of juicy nicknames – most of his longstanding admirers probably suppose they could guess what kind of celebratory evening he enjoyed after such a dramatic Old Firm derby, but again they would be wrong. However, to begin at the beginning, the Nicholas story started in Cowcaddens, the tenement district in the heart of Glasgow which was swept away so completely in the city's passion to build motorways and high rise flats that almost all that survives is the name of the subway station round the corner from the Theatre Royal and the studios of Scottish Television.

Nicholas was born on 30 December 1961 into an area which was as hard-bitten as any in Glasgow and, of course, as sharp-witted. When razor gangs resurfaced to shame the city later in the Sixties, the Cowcaddens crew called themselves the Shamrock, after the street of that name, now long demolished. Younger mental cases who were considered too junior to be full Shamrock members were known as the BabySham.

The Nicholas family poured its enthusiasm into the more acceptable activity of following Celtic with a passion. Charlie's father Chic (at this point it is tempting to switch into Stanley Baxter's *Parliamo Glasgow* mode – 'Chic Nic'n'Charlie Nic oan a picnic!') was himself the son of a man known for making the long walk to Celtic Park. Chic made the journey in more comfortable circumstances, on the supporters' bus from the Station Bar in Port Dundas Road, one Cowcaddens establishment which is still on the go.

When, in due course, Charlie took his place on the bus he had the company of a boy three years older, who lived next door. His name, Jim Duffy, was also destined to become well-known to Celtic supporters. 'Me and James went everywhere. We were two pals and at the age of five I was going to the Celtic end with him.'

When Cowcaddens was redeveloped the Nicholas family moved three miles north-west to what the Corporation housing department liked to call the Wyndford Estate but which was known to everyone else in Maryhill as the Barracks, because it was built inside the boundary wall of the old Army depot which once confined Rudolph Hess after the deputy Fuhrer of Nazi Germany had parachuted into Scotland with the idea of solving World War II.

Nicholas and Duffy discovered a handy alternative to Celtic in the local Junior side, who played a couple of hundred yards away at Lochburn Park. Maryhill FC were an old established club, founded in 1884, with an impressive record of generating talent for the Old Firm. Davie Mieklejohn, rated by some as the greatest ever captain of Rangers, had been a Maryhill player, but it was Celtic who got the benefit of a fine harvest in the Seventies when they recruited Danny McGrain, Tommy Burns and Paul Wilson.

'I used to watch the Juniors a lot,' Nicholas remembers. 'Maryhill had a good team then, a real skilful side and to be honest most of the ambition for James and me at the time was to play for them. James eventually fulfilled that but I never did, although I played against them a good few times for Celtic youths. I went to Lochburn Park a lot on Sundays and if Celtic weren't playing on Saturdays I would watch the Thistle if they were at Firhill. We used to climb over the wall from the canal bank but that stopped when we got chased by the Maryhill Team.'

To which one can only add that the Maryhill Team must have been a seriously slow gang if Charlie Nicholas was able to outrun them. Persuaded by this stroke of fate to keep clear of Partick Thistle, Nicholas confined his attentions to Celtic and his first clear recollection of a game at Celtic Park is Tommy Gemmell's spectacular opening goal in the 3–0 victory over Benfica in a second round, first leg tie in November 1969. 'The first vivid memory I do recall from any game is that goal by Tommy Gemmell. I think it must have been a 30-yarder but in my estimation that night it was a 70-yarder. It was just one of the strangest and most exciting things I had seen in my youth and it will always stay with me, that memory, because afterwards there was no way I was going to stop watching Celtic.'

Oddly, Nicholas was playing with Rangers Boys' Club in Drumchapel on Saturday afternoons after turning out in the morning for the mixed religion side composed of youngsters from St Gregory's Primary and Wyndford Primary, two schools inside the Barracks. 'We joined forces and I used to turn out for the mixed school. When I was ten years old I went to Celtic and had trials and eventually got through but I had my ups and downs with the Boys' Club, to be honest. There was a period at under-14 level when I wasn't growing, except maybe outwards rather than upwards, and they were playing me at right wing. Well, I've never been known for my pace so gradually I was slipping out of the team to the point where I was very close to packing it in.'

The change of fortune occurred in the under-16 side when Nicholas was switched from sweeper, another unsuitable role, to forward. Within three months Nicholas played trials with Bobby Robson's Ipswich and Manchester City. When Sammy Chung, then the Wolves manager, offered the teenager a contract on his first day at Molyneux it dawned on Celtic that they had better move swiftly or lose an increasingly prominent talent. On the recommendation of Frank Cairney – and against the judgment of Dave McParland, the Celtic assistant manager – Jock Stein agreed to sign Nicholas.

He scored in a Glasgow Cup game against Queen's Park and, on 22 August 1979, made his first home appearance in a semi-final against Clyde when he again netted in a 3–0 victory. Then it was into the reserves to learn a professional's trade for the rest of the 1979–80 season, at the end of which Alex Ferguson's Aberdeen had deprived Celtic of their status as champions. The rise of Aberdeen and Dundee United earned the north-east clubs the title of the New Firm and the 1980–81 championship became a race between Celtic and Aberdeen.

By April, when Celtic prepared to travel to Ibrox for the final Old Firm game of the season six points ahead of Aberdeen with four matches remaining, it was clear that they were within touching distance of the flag. The position was that if Celtic beat

Rangers they would be champions in all but name, even if Aberdeen beat Airdrie at Pittodrie because Aberdeen had a much poorer goal difference. If Aberdeen and Celtic should both lose their games the position would be the same and, of course, if Celtic were to gain any more points on Aberdeen then Billy McNeill's players would be champions officially.

At this stage Nicholas had established himself in the Celtic first team and he had already discovered that a Glasgow derby is an unforgiving fixture. 'I always had a natural talent and after leaving Frank Cairney's side I was in the under-18 youth team, by which time I was also on the ground staff under big Billy. I think they had seen immediately that there was something in me which could progress quite quickly because I was only on the ground staff for three or four months. There were a few injuries in the reserves and I ended up playing reserve football before I had signed pro forms.

'I was up front with Tom McAdam and in my first game we scored two each. From then on it just snowballed and I was on the bench at first team games within three months. The next season – 1980–81 – I really got into the team on a regular basis and although I missed the first Old Firm game of the season when we beat Rangers 2–1 at Celtic Park, Billy put me in for the next one at Ibrox. That turned out to be a personal nightmare because we lost 3–0 and I had no experience of anything like that atmosphere so that the whole thing just ran by me.

'But when we played them at home again in February I scored two, which did a lot for my confidence and settled me down, so I think when it came to the game in April I was ready for it. I had gathered a wee bit experience, a wee bit of knowledge, but the big thing was that we were going for the title and the atmosphere had been brewing up for weeks. I had won honours all my days with the boys' clubs and it had always been easy but this was so much more spectacular, a championship with Celtic.'

The Celtic support had readily seen that Nicholas was one of them, a true player for the jersey out of the tradition of cavalier forward play, with a reputation that could only have been magnified by his goals against Rangers – and his vivacious response whenever he put the ball behind an opposing goalkeeper. Certainly, for Nicholas there was a powerful sense of bonding with the fans he had so recently stood alongside.

'As you say, the rapport I had with the crowd was just fantastic.

To say that I used to go home and shake myself would be an understatement. When I got in my father would stand there and kill himself laughing because the kids surrounded me coming in the door and I would be on the doorstep for ages. So there was this extraordinary glamour but life at home was going on the same as it had when I was a supporter.

'To give you an example of what the contrast was like, on a match day I might be playing in front of, say, 60,000 at Celtic Park but before Danny McGrain would pick me up at the Barracks gates my father, who did the cooking in our house, would make my pre-match meal. Nowadays you hear about protein diets or pasta diets or players eating fruit and bran but my pre-match meal was three hot dogs and my father would have them cooked for me and see me out the door before he got ready to go to the game. It's ridiculous really when you think about it.

'Before the championship game at Ibrox there was such excitement building up, not only in the press and television and radio – reporters were never away from Celtic and Rangers that week – but also amongst the family and friends. My father was getting more and more nervous as the days went by and on the Thursday evening he went out to his local, the Politician in Maryhill Road, for a couple of pints. When he came in I said to him to make sure he had the hot dogs ready before the game, which just got him worse because at the best of times he liked to prepare everything a day in advance. My mother Rina was a bag of nerves and she couldn't sleep at all at nights, so there was some atmosphere in our house.

'We're not superstitious but it had got to the stage that I just said: "Same'll do me, dad," so it was the three hot dogs, out and meet Danny and away we went.'

Old Firm games had only recently emerged from a menacing passage in their history, culminating in the Hampden Riot of 1980, when fighting supporters clashed on the pitch of the national stadium after George McCluskey's goal had given Celtic a 1–0 win in the Scottish Cup final. The consequence was the rapid introduction of the Criminal Justice (Scotland) Act which made it illegal to be in possession of alcohol in Scottish football grounds or to be under the influence of drink.

The arrest rate fell dramatically at a fixture which was a byword for trouble throughout Britain and abroad, not that the tradition of enjoying a pre-match aperitif was dented and the atmosphere at Old Firm collisions were still on the raw side, particularly amongst Rangers fans who had seen Celtic win the title in a stunning finale to the 1978–79 season with a 4–2 victory at home and who were not overjoyed at the prospect of another green and white triumph, especially if it was to be played out at Ibrox. There were early signs for Nicholas that there might be a somewhat fraught afternoon ahead.

'I was quite nervy, to be honest, because there was a lot of bad blood in the air coming up to this game, as there had been through that period for a number of years, usually with crowd disturbances and the like. It was highlighted just after Danny picked me up. I was pretty quiet, which is unusual for me, and Danny was doing most of the nattering. He was saying that I shouldn't worry too much and that whether or not we won today we could do it at Dundee United in the next game and anyway Aberdeen might slip up, whereas I could only think that it would be wonderful to win the league at Ibrox – it really would be amazing.

'There had been warnings in the newspapers that morning that if any player scored a goal they had better watch out how they celebrated it because of the tension in the air. So everybody was made aware of that side of the proceedings. We had only got just past the Eastpark Home on Maryhill Road when we had to stop at traffic lights and there was a wee gang of Rangers supporters, about eight of them, making their way to one of the local boozers before they got the bus.

'They noticed Danny and me right away and we got a bit of verbal from them. Danny being his usual self just flicked it off and got on with his driving and I was smirking, but quite nervous just the same. By then you could feel that, yes, today there was something special happening.'

Any footballer will testify to the strange change of temperament which can overtake players on the lead-up to a very important game. Chatty individuals become sombre and withdrawn while the quiet ones often start to rabbit. This is the moment when everyone becomes grateful to the lads who are able to treat the occasion as though it was just another Saturday. 'Danny and Frank McGarvey, who was usually bubbly, kept things going – George McCluskey, too – but some of the others had gone quiet like myself and big Packie Bonner, up the back of the bus. Dom Sullivan was there, although he didn't play, but when we talk about the ones who really help the dressing-room, people like Dom are essential.

'He was a guy who seemed to love every minute he was involved with Celtic even when he wasn't playing, which I find so hard. When I'm not involved I have trouble getting my personality across but Dom was bubbling away and he was a major help. I don't even like going out for warm-ups when I'm playing, even though when I got older I had to start doing it properly to make sure that the muscles would be working properly.

'I felt that two o'clock was about the time I should be starting my routine. When I first started at the pro game I used to watch Danny McGrain and his habits and he would get under way at two o'clock or earlier, putting the strapping on his ankles, getting his massage early, putting on his boots so his feet would have adjusted by the time the game got going. So I watched him carefully, taking it in, doing those things, but the excitement outside and the warm-ups, no. If somebody was having a laugh or cracking a light I would like to be involved in it but when it came to quarter to three it was serious stuff. You knew you had to buckle down then, especially with a championship at stake.'

There was no shortage of leaders in the camp, McGrain and Roy Aitken prominent amongst them, and Billy McNeill inspiring the side before the task which was about to begin. Nicholas noticed one significant difference about McNeill's final talk that afternoon.

'I think it was the first time I noticed that it wasn't about Rangers in any way. It was all about us, how if we could go out and play in our own way with guys like Provan and Burns and MacLeod, who had been scoring goals, we would have more than enough to give them problems. And I felt exactly that because the thought of winning the league would give us the extra adrenalin we needed to do our job properly.

'I had no preference about which end we should shoot into because it just gets to the stage at Ibrox, even more so now, that it's such a daunting place you have to say to yourself: 'I just want to play here – this is what being a top footballer is all about.' As soon as you fear it, it'll slap you right between the eyes and afterwards I thought, never again. I'll never go back there and worry about it.'

Watch an Old Firm game and if 15 seconds pass without a foul, you're probably witnessing a contest of exceptional fluency. Everyone is braced for the first slap and every player is anxious to make a good first contact with the ball. 'Most of my first touches were from Danny McGrain passes and he did it again that afternoon,' Nicholas says. 'Danny took it over the halfway line and dinked a little ten-yard curler in towards me. My first touch, which tends to set my mind at ease if it is good because of the kind of player I am, was straight into Davie Provan's path first time. It set us off on a sweeping attack right away because Danny immediately overlapped Davie and we got a corner. Nothing came of the corner, but I remember it so well because I thought to myself, I'm off to a good start, and I thought automatically that the team was off to a good start as well, which is as much as you need in an Old Firm game.'

Now, given Charlie Nicholas's claims for this match – simply the best team performance he encountered, with Celtic or any other club – it seems surprising that reports of the game portray it as a scrappy and tough affair. The midfield dogfight was typified by repeated fouls and flare-ups and Jim Bett of Rangers was booked after he had clattered both Burns and MacLeod. There were no goals to enliven the action before half-time. How does that square with the claim of a superlative team game?

'I just felt that we had so much of the play that day, we were passing well, we were calm, we were composed and we were playing the ball around at the back. I know we weren't as cavalier as we would have liked to be and as we usually were at that time, but we all realised without really saying anything about it to each other that on this occasion what really mattered was to stay in control of the occasion and to solve each problem as it came along. We paced the game so well and we kept on making such good situations to vary the game, with Danny surging down the right and Davie Provan taking the ball off for a walk so that the rest of us could have a breather for 15 or 20 seconds.

'I could see everybody playing very well without anyone being real stars and it seemed to me when it finished that not one of us was tired as we walked off the pitch. I looked all around at our faces and I thought, hey, we controlled this game so easily. We had been playing a lot of keep-ball, me and Frank McGarvey, and it was just one of those days where everything was coming off, all the first time stuff.

'Even after 15 minutes or so we could feel the frustration coming down from the Rangers supporters. The Rangers players were getting in about us, they were trying to give us a few heavy slaps, which they did, but I could sense the frustration amongst them too, as well as the whole Rangers crowd bracing themselves because they knew we would probably beat them that day.

'When Rangers came off at half-time you could really see the strain in their faces. They knew they were having a lot of trouble keeping the lid on the game and they needed help which, of course, our supporters were making sure they wouldn't get. Our lot were going berserk up their end and to me the Rangers players all had the look of knowing that this was becoming reality, that we would win the title at their place, which they didn't fancy one bit but couldn't do anything about.'

Still, as the second half got under way, all the signs were that both teams would settle for a scoreless draw: Rangers because in that event Celtic would have to go off and win their championship somewhere else and Celtic because it would put the title almost beyond dispute.

'In such circumstances as these,' wrote Alan Davidson in the *Evening Times*, 'with both sides intent on giving nothing away, it was always going to take a special player to breach the defences. Celtic certainly have one in their precocious teenager, Charlie Nicholas.

'When few of the crowd were betting on any goals being scored, Nicholas conjured up a superb effort to put his side in front after 56 minutes, and so closer to the title.

'The young striker coolly collected a Davie Provan pass before slipping his shot past Stewart, with all the calm of a player who had been in the game a lifetime.'

According to Nicholas, Provan was the architect of the goal from the start of the build-up. 'Well, it was mainly Davie deep in his own half and he kept coming on, eventually having a run at a couple of defenders and then cut inside along the edge of the box, going in central, and I had pulled out slightly to the right while Frank McGarvey had moved in along with Davie for a one-two.

'But Davie had angled the pass outside the goal and I just took it in my stride with my left peg and pinged it inside the far post. Actually, it hit the back stanchion and bounced along the net. It was probably as sweet a strike as I ever had off my left foot but it was the result of a wonderful run by Davie, who must have taken four players with him to make the space. I still had a lot of work to do because it was an 18-yard angled shot but it was thanks to Davie and Frank, both of them making room for me, that I had the chance to take it.'

At this supreme moment of his good fortune, Rangers may have had nowhere to hide but Nicholas had nowhere to run. 'I was in a crazy situation because I should explain that before the match started the referee, Brian McGinlay – who I felt was one of the best referees I've ever had and certainly at that time was the best in the country – had warned us all beforehand that if we scored into the Rangers end we were not to dare to do anything to provoke them. If we did, we would get a yellow card or worse.

'Danny McGrain then said to me: "You heard what he said, so be careful, be really careful." As soon as I had scored the goal, which was at the Rangers end, I turned to run because I was surrounded on three sides by Rangers supporters but I had nowhere obvious to go so I headed towards the main stand and Danny McGrain was there. I jumped up on Danny and he got me in a bear hug and carried me off back to the halfway line, so that we didn't do anything to the Rangers supporters to provoke them.

'When I look back on it now I think, by God, Danny was shrewd, even in a tense situation like that he was clever again, grabbing me straight back to our half. And I've never heard the Rangers end so quiet – I mean *quiet*!'

Not that Rangers or their supporters stayed hushed for long. Whichever side goes behind in an Old Firm derby will usually reach into the tank for a mighty effort to turn the game around and so Rangers did as Celtic concentrated on holding on to the precious advantage conferred by Nicholas's superb strike. For about quarter of an hour the blue jerseys surged down upon Bonner and Robert Russell hit the bar with a dangerous effort. Roy Aitken cleared off the line and the blue tide began to ebb.

At last Brian McGinlay blew full-time and mindful of the referee's warnings the Celtic players restrained their celebrations, keeping to the halfway line and briefly acknowledging the supporters who were bouncing in ecstasy amidst a green and white sea while the rest of ground quickly emptied. In those days there were no tunnel extensions to shield the players as they came off, so the smart move was to sprint through the venom for the safety of the dressing-room.

Where the exultant Celtic board had laid on champagne in anticipation of another league triumph? Er, not exactly. This was a previous generation of Celtic directors, remember, so it looked as though the celebration would lose its sparkle almost before it had begun. Except that one man could be relied upon never to let the Celtic players down . . . Jimmy Steele, Celtic masseur and an extraordinary individual, a reputed millionaire from wartime business activities and a fan who insisted on working for nothing, a trait which must have doubly endeared him to the old regime at Celtic Park.

'Jimmy Steele, probably the greatest man I ever met in my life, came to the rescue as usual. Sure, we had a few cans of beer around but suddenly Jimmy, who was cracking his jokes and fooling around like he always did, rummled around in his bag and pulled out a couple of bottles of champagne. So we opened them and away we went, not that we drank much of it, just sprayed it around the place. But that was it, the moment had been reached.'

Then the coach ride back to Celtic Park, a minute or two to mingle with the well wishers waiting back at the ground and then it was home or, in the case of Nicholas & Co., off to Glasgow city centre and a licensed establishment called Archie's which was the venue for serious post-match analysis and light-hearted refreshments – or vice versa?

'We would talk about good games, talk about bad games, it didn't make any difference. What was really happening – and I noticed it particularly in my first season – was that this social scene brought us all together. We would be in for a couple of pints, usually even the guys who were married, before they would meet their wives at about seven or eight o'clock and then we would all go our separate ways. I would wait on my pals coming, who were Danny Crainie, Willie McStay and Mick Conroy, who was part of the group that night obviously, and we were the single guys so we could stay out late and play.'

There would be similar scenes later in the Nicholas saga when he was an Arsenal player, although Tramps and Annabel's stood in for Archie's. Before the move to London, though, Nicholas was to win another championship medal with Celtic in 1981–82 and scored Celtic's first goal in the 2–1 League Cup final victory over Rangers in December 1982. He netted 28 goals in 45 matches in his rookie season, with three against Rangers including the strike which took the flag to Celtic Park, and achieved an extraordinary 46 goals in 52 games two years later. Even in 1981–82 when he broke his leg playing for the reserves against Morton he still ran up half a dozen goals in 14 games, 11 of which he started.

Perhaps he was bound to leave Glasgow because although he loves the city – and anyone who knows him well will testify to his willingness to volunteer his attachment to the Dear Green Place –

he could never have been nicknamed Cheapskate Charlie; his first spell with Celtic coincided with a wages policy which could not contain his estimate of his own worth. He moved to Highbury on 22 June 1983 for £750,000 and in January 1988 went from Arsenal to Aberdeen in a £450,000 deal. They were not barren years by any measure.

For Arsenal he scored 34 goals in 151 league games and both goals in the Gunners' victory over Liverpool at Wembley in the 1987 Littlewoods Cup final. With Aberdeen he won a Skol Cup medal against Rangers in October 1989 and a Scottish Cup medal against Celtic in 1990. In fact, his last kick of the ball for Aberdeen was to beat Packie Bonner in the 1990 Scottish Cup final penalty decider.

The Arsenal fans revered him. He left Aberdeen with good wishes from their supporters and he he was greeted with approval by Celtic fans when he returned to Parkhead for a second spell that summer. Nevertheless, most Celtic people are of the opinion that he might have done better in the 15 years which elapsed between rattling the stanchion in the Rangers net at Ibrox and the casual nutmeg on Gazza at Broadwood. In particular, they believe that if he had to leave Paradise it should have been for Liverpool rather than London.

To this day Charlie also has ambivalent feelings about the path of his career. 'As you quite rightly say, Arsenal was strange for me because I was adored by the majority of the Arsenal supporters. Considering what I was going through they were tremendous. I was going through a real up and down time with my form and the team was much the same. I always found it strange, when it comes to the crunch, how those London people could look upon me like that. I mean I'm a Glasgow boy, born in the city, I'm a true Glaswegian and I'm very proud of being a Glaswegian. As far as football goes, everything about me has been Celtic and through my mid-twenties I always wondered how the Arsenal fans could have such a feeling for me when I didn't really support their club.

'Whereas I'd always been brought up with Celtic and the club represented my affinity and my real beliefs and I suppose my expressions when I scored for Celtic during my first period told the fans that I was definitely a Celtic man. I had the same anxiety about Aberdeen because I don't think I ever made a secret about where my heart really lies. And yet the Aberdeen supporters always knew what I was and accepted it and I am very grateful to them for that.

'What I did find hard was to come back to Celtic because by that time it turned out to be a club which was going in a direction which wasn't suiting anybody connected with it, so that there was a lot of bad feeling in the air between directors and supporters. There were players including myself who never put their proper form together and a good few of us would ask ourselves if this was really the place we had been brought up to love. And it was definitely not, as events proved.'

Even then Nicholas was still capable of unearthing a nugget from the dross, like the dazzling strike which set Celtic on the way to a 2–0 Easter derby win over Rangers at Ibrox in 1992. But there were to be no championships for Celtic during that unhappy era and no more Champagne Charlie headlines, on or off the field, because by then he had settled down with his wife Claire to bring up two daughters Nadine and Sophie.

To be fair to Nicholas, he insists on setting the record straight about his motives for choosing Arsenal when he departed Celtic Park for the first time. 'I kept reading the same story, that I was leaving for the bright lights and the high living but that was nonsense. I didn't know what existed in London – I soon found out, right enough – but I had only been there once and that was to watch Scotland get hammered 5–1 by the English and I had never been there socially.

'Arsenal were a major club who hadn't won anything for a while and who told me that they were going to buy Liam Brady back, a genius of a player, as well as two or three other real stars. I felt they were going to be very ambitious. In the end they failed to get any of these players and at the age of 21 I became the guy who was going to be the saviour and it turned out to be wrong, but only in football terms.

'Liverpool would have been the right one for me. As far as Arsenal are concerned I can't say anything else negative about that club. However, nothing can ever compare with playing for Celtic and the pinnacle of all the performances for me must be the '81 championship match.'

Finally, then, what was the climax of that celebratory evening, when the teenage Championship Charlie went on the town with his team-mates?

'Well, only Mick Conroy had a house of his own as a single boy, out in Bishopton and occasionally we used to go back there but most of the time we weren't using his place we would go back to my parents in Maryhill. My father was on night shift so by the time we were coming back in after the game at Ibrox my father was just getting home as well.

'He had a couple of bevvies in him but as usual he served up the home made soup and all the guys had their stuff. Then we all had a few more bevvies and we did what we usually did. We all went to sleep on the floor.'

As they say in Glasgow – aw, the nice . . .

Davie Provan

DUNDALK 0 CELTIC 0

7 November 1979

OVER the nine years that Davie Provan played for Celtic there
was not a defender in Scotland who would deny his ability to
wrongfoot opponents, but it was not only on the pitch that Provan
managed to confound expectations about him. He was a Rangers
supporter whose ambition was to wear the light blue jersey, yet he
became such a favourite with the Celtic supporters that 45,000 of
them turned up at his testimonial match against Nottingham
Forest in 1987, an occasion which also saw Kenny Dalglish make
a guest appearance for his former club in honour of Provan.

He was a supremely fit footballer whose career was cut short by
a mysterious viral illness which one doctor – in Provan's presence
on a networked television broadcast – dismissed as being an
excuse for malingering. The illness, known as ME, is now
recognised as a condition which can amount to serious disability
for some of its sufferers.

Every Celtic fan who was present at the 1985 Scottish Cup final
victory over Dundee United will remember how the game was
turned in Celtic's favour in the closing stages by an exquisite free
kick by Provan. He was the Scottish Professional Footballers
Association's Player of the Year in 1980 and he made ten
appearances for Scotland, yet the game which remains foremost in
his mind from his playing days is a relatively obscure fixture
against Dundalk, a part-time League of Ireland club. To complete
a portrait of contrasts, this gifted attacker has chosen as his most
memorable match a contest which produced no goals.

Davie Provan was a Gourock boy who started with a local junior
side, Port Glasgow, and was signed by Kilmarnock in 1974. Billy

McNeill had played against him and was an admirer of his bewildering trickery on the ball, so within a few months of succeeding Jock Stein as manager in 1978 McNeill moved for Provan. He demonstrated his belief in the player's abilities by paying £125,000 which was then the record fee for a transfer between two Scottish clubs, not that the move was greeted with rapture in the Provan household.

'I was an out and out Rangers supporter who came from a Rangers-daft household,' Provan confesses. 'My brother was a Rangers fanatic, my dad was a Rangers man, we used to go to Ibrox when I was young and that, I suppose, was the irony when I ended up signing for Celtic. My brother wasn't very happy about it, I can tell you, and I lost some friends as well – in retrospect friends I didn't need – but it was very strange to go from being a complete Rangers fan as a boy to playing in so many Old Firm matches as a Celtic player and really enjoy beating them, actually loving the moment.

'It's a strange one, the first time you pull on the Celtic jersey to play against Rangers, if you've supported the other side. Even when I was with Kilmarnock I felt it when we played them. But the minute you pull on a Celtic jersey, there's a switch which is pulled and the first time you run out in front of the Celtic supporters you realise your obligations and the aspirations they have for the club.

'It takes you a long time to realise what it's really all about to play for them, it's something that you have to grow into. Eventually you become aware that along with Rangers it's a very special institution in Scotland and there is a huge amount of responsibility on you to give your lot for these people and that's the only way you can stay at Celtic for any length of time.

'I don't think I could ever have done what Mo did and cross to the other side once I was established at Celtic, even though I had a Rangers background. I think Mo's the only one mad enough to do it. A lot of people would say that he did it for the money but knowing Mo he probably did it just to be the first – or at least the most controversial – and he is fearless. It didn't surprise me greatly because when all the rumours were circulating and I would be asked if I thought it was possible I said, well, definitely, because I know the guy.

'It took an awful lot of bottle to do it – and madness as well – but he did it.'

We can assume that it was wiser for Davie Provan not to go into too many details about his background for the benefit of the Celtic supporters after his arrival because it was almost inevitable that Provan would become a swift favourite of theirs. He was a classic Scottish winger cast from an old fashioned mould – a species which is almost extinct today – and he usually performed as an outside right, spinning markers like tops as they tried to pen him in against the touchline. His crosses into the box were a delight and his repertoire was completed by a modern touch, the Rivelino-style command of free kicks which would curl the ball around defensive walls and goalkeepers alike.

A year after he signed for Celtic he was a fixture in the first team and already had a championship medal, secured in the sensational 4–2 victory over Rangers in the final match of the previous season. So why does the game against Dundalk stay so vivid in his memory?

Says Provan: 'The answer is that it was the strangest match I ever played in and although a lot of people may not remember it much today, it came close to being one of the worst results in our history. Of course, being a European Cup-tie it was played over two legs and the story really starts with the first game in Glasgow. This was the second round of the tournament and it was generally reckoned to be a great draw for us.

'We had played Partisan Tirana in the first round and although they beat us 1–0 over there in Albania and also scored in the return at Celtic Park we had come through that one pretty comfortably. So everybody looked at the draw and thought, fine, a part-time team from the League of Ireland. Obviously we were expected to get through and the players certainly expected to get through but the first leg turned out to be a very, very tricky game for us. We won 3–2 but they were a far better side than we had anticipated and we were fortunate to get a victory.

'Looking back, I really don't know how it happened. Billy McNeill had said on the Monday before the game that providing we prepared for it mentally in the correct way and if we played the match at our pace, so that we were always in control, we would get the job done. I dare say we must still have underestimated them and although it sounded ridiculous then, a part-time team from a league which was nothing like the standard of ours turned out on the night at Celtic Park to be a very accomplished side.

'They opened us up so many times that night and had so many

good chances that they really should have beaten us. They were a capable side, a lot of experience amongst them and they also had a couple of tricky players, a combination which will cause you problems if you aren't properly attuned to dealing with it, and we ended up walking a tightrope in the second leg.

'But it was the next morning that the psychology of their manager Jimmy McLaughlin really started because he had claimed that his players had got in at four o'clock on the morning of the game, that they had been sampling the Guinness in some decent Glasgow hostelries and that they would follow the same routine for the second leg. All of which added to the pressure on us for the second leg because our supporters were far from pleased at the display we had put up in the first game and they had booed us off the field at full-time.

'When they found out – or, at least, were led to believe – that we had scraped through against a bunch of part-timers who had been out on the bevvy for most of the night before the game, in their view it made us look a pretty poor lot.

'Jimmy was at it again before the second leg, saying that this game was for the Catholic championship of the world. He tried to trivialise it, which suited his lads and kept stepping up the pressure we felt. His idea was to get people to believe that it didn't matter to them, whereas we needed to get a good result.Anyway, for the second game in Dundalk we made our way over and stayed in the Ballymascanlon House Hotel, which was just outside the town and meant to be the usual kind of base for us, a quiet spot where we could keep ourselves to ourselves as much as possible.

'From the moment we arrived we were invaded – and that is the only word for it, because it never stopped – by supporters and well-wishers. Such was the team's popularity in Ireland that we were a tourist attraction and the hotel was besieged by people wanting photographs and autographs, so it became increasingly difficult to prepare properly. The demand for tickets was so huge that there had been suggestions that the game might be moved to Lansdowne Road in Dublin but the club wanted to keep the game in Dundalk and actually rebuilt part of the ground to accommodate some of the supporters who were clamouring to get in.

'For those who are not familiar with Dundalk, it should be mentioned that it is very close to the border with Northern Ireland where, of course, Celtic have a lot of support and all of that just added to the pressure on the club to play the match in front of as big a crowd as possible. The directors were obviously going for the big financial kill and the bulldozers were in during the week of the tie to clear the way for temporary seating to be put in place.

'The night of the game arrived and I remember the road to the stadium very well because we had police motorcycle escorts who in typical Irish tradition actually drove behind the bus. So we had the bus, with two motorcycle riders trailing along after us, trying to move through these crowds of people streaming through the streets of Dundalk, all trying to get to Oriel Park where the game was being played.

'At one stage we thought that we were going to be late for the kick-off but we made it eventually with time to spare. However, when we got there we simply couldn't believe what we were seeing. The place was like a construction site, which was actually what it had been for several days before the match, and the bulldozers had been all over the pitch, which was the worst I've seen in my life.

'There was a band up on a stand in the centre circle and they were all having the time of their life while here we were on the really serious business of trying to get through to the last eight of the European Cup which, as we would soon find out, would bring us up against Real Madrid in the quarter-finals. We were all feeling the pressure. I remember Billy McNeill, who could by and large mask his tension at times of stress, showing obvious strain on his face. It was the first experience I had ever had of the type of pressure you can be under as an Old Firm player and how very hard it can be to cope with.

'We got into the dressing-room and, as you know, in Britain and in most other countries, the dressing-room is sacrosanct. Nobody gets in the dressing-room, not even the chairman, the directors – nobody. Billy started his final talk but before he could get properly into it he was interrupted – and he kept on being interrupted – by Irish people continually walking in with cameras and asking us to pose for pictures, wee boys being brought in and introduced to the players by these Dundalk supporters who were just delighted because Celtic were in town.

'It was the most bizarre way to go into a European tie and it was obvious we were never going to get a minute's peace in this tiny little dressing-room. Eventually, big Billy threw the hamper against the door and John Clark sat on it so that nobody else could interrupt us.'

McNeill's agitation was understandable and as the late Hugh

Taylor, writing next day in the *Evening Times* put it: 'Manager McNeill realised it was not to be the usual European Cup-tie, the usual game of patience, of leisurely movement and sophisticated tactics.

'He knew Dundalk, on their night of nights, would play fiercely and heroically if not scientifically, digging in with all the subtlety of a bash from a shillelagh. And so it proved.'

Provan takes up the story again: 'When we were ready to start, with everybody psyched up for what we knew now was going to be a very difficult tie we went out into the tunnel area and it was absolute bedlam.

'The referee, who was Danish, couldn't believe his eyes because this band was going on and on in the centre circle. The Danish guy was trying to explain to the Dundalk officials that this was a European Cup match and it had to kick off on time. So the stage was hastily dismantled, the teams took to the terrible pitch and right from the word go we knew we were going to be in for a torrid night because we hadn't put in the work we should have done in Glasgow.

'There was a crowd of 16,000 or so, most of whom I suspect wanted Celtic to win. They were almost all Irish but most of them were Celtic supporters. Actually, the atmosphere was very odd from our point of view and to be honest, between the state of the pitch and the temporary seating which I doubt very much was safe, the game should never have been allowed and wouldn't be nowadays with those arrangements. Not that we could blame Dundalk, because they were obviously going for the big money hit and I think their gate receipts were £38,000 which was four times as much as they had ever taken at the gate.

'They came out of it with a few quid and we came out of it with shredded nerves, I'm afraid. There were times you had to rub your eyes to believe what you were seeing. There were dogs coming on, cats, people on and off the pitch – one lot were dancing on the grass – and it was just one of those crazy, crazy nights. They got the local parish priest out of the stand at half-time to appeal to people to stay off the field of play.

'This is why it sticks out in my memory so much because in the next round we were in the Bernabeu Stadium against Real Madrid and there could hardly be a more stark contrast between Madrid and Oriel Park, but that's European football for you – you go where you're sent. Had it been a pre-season tour, and we had a few of those in Ireland, it would have been great because you can relax and enjoy the hospitality and say hello to all the people who just want to be around Celtic, but that night it really was an encumbrance and something we could all have done without and we were just very glad to get back home with the result having gone the right way.

'We had what I thought was a good goal disallowed for offside early on and when we got to half-time it was 0–0. There had been one or two scares but we were pretty well in control of the match. Then it was back to the dressing-room and this time Billy was determined that we would be the only people inside, so it was the hamper against the door again.

'But I do remember a wee Irish guy getting in. We're trying to get our act together at half-time, still on a tightrope, and this little guy came in, at which point Billy lost his temper and grabbed him bodily, chucked him out and slammed the door. I think from then on the lads who were queuing up to get into our dressing-room got the message that they were not exactly welcome at that time.

'Once we were barricaded in I remember him saying that we had actually played well enough in the first half but that because Dundalk were operating a pretty effective offside trap he wanted the midfield players to try to get forward. We were using a 3–4–3 system which was meant to take advantage of their tactics and Bobby Lennox and I were supposed to use our speed to get past them on the wings but they were quick to come out when the ball was knocked forward to us. So we needed the front players to concentrate on staying onside and knock the ball over the top to allow our midfield players to get in behind them.

'But Dundalk were very sharp at operating the offside trap and their captain, Dermot Keeley, played at the back and used his experience to marshal their back four very well. They made it difficult for us all night.

'I think I felt the pressure particularly because I had only been at Celtic Park about 14 months at that time and I was going through a good spell, so a lot was expected of me. I was supposed to open teams up but the pitch at Oriel Park was so tight and bumpy and Dundalk gave us no room at all, they pushed right up to the halfway line to squeeze the game and gave us no time, so I managed to get a couple of half decent crosses into the box but it wasn't a particularly productive night for me.

'When we went out again for the second half, as so often happens in a match like that you start to protect what you have and you become more uptight and more nervous. We just had to dig in and grind at it. I don't care if you're Celtic, Real Madrid or anyone else, when you go to a ground like that and defend a one-goal lead it's invariably difficult. There is always going to be a chance for the other side and Dundalk's opportunity came with about two minutes left. It fell to a lad called Liam Devine, an inside forward.

'They broke down the left for them and hit a great ball across the face of the goal, and it was an easy chance – six yards out with Peter Latchford on his line and plenty of time to take it – so when I saw it happen I thought, that's it, we're out. You could just see the headlines next day – Celtic Dumped By Part Timers – and then it would be the Jimmy McLaughlin show all over, telling the world they'd been out on the piss again before the game and warning Real Madrid that they were playing for the Catholic championship of the world.

'But the poor lad took his eye off the ball and let it run under his foot. He missed the chance, thank goodness for us.

'At that moment we realised we were through and we did hold out until full-time but it was the most nerve-wracking night of my Celtic career. Afterwards I had a drink with Martin Lawlor, their full back, and he told me that they had never been on the town in Glasgow. They had been tucked up in bed at ten o'clock the night before the game, but when Jimmy McLaughlin gave out that they were on the bevvy it was just his way of putting pressure on us, and you would have to say that it worked to a fair degree.

'I was never in any hurry to go back to Oriel Park and certainly not to get into that kind of situation again, not that we had any problem with Jimmy or his players or any of the Dundalk folk for that matter. In fact, when we went back to the Ballymascanlon House Hotel after the match some of the Dundalk players came with us and it was only then for the first time we could relax and enjoy the hospitality. There were a few pints of Guinness sunk that night and in our case it was mainly with relief.'

There was another reason for profound gratitude that the game had passed with nothing more sinister than a large ration of eccentricity to make it memorable. In recent weeks there had been serious sectarian violence at games in the north and there was a deep-seated fear that with a Republic of Ireland club playing Celtic, the prospect of a double target might cause loyalist attacks to spill across the border.

'I think Billy McNeill had been involved in talks with the local police and the security forces but to be fair to him he never mentioned any of that to us and he kept it all well in the background, which must have added to the strain he was feeling. The last thing we needed to think about was the troubles in the north and it was something which never really entered into the reckoning,' is Provan's recollection.

Having survived the numerous traps laid for them by the wily Jimmy McLaughlin, Celtic could pass the winter months in pleasant contemplation of their quarter-final encounter with the champions of Spain. When they met Real Madrid before a 67,000 crowd at Celtic Park on 5 March 1980 they gave themselves an excellent chance of reaching the last four with a 2–0 win with goals from George McCluskey and Johnny Doyle. The return leg, before 110,000 spectators at the Bernabeu Stadium was a world away from Oriel Perk.

Unfortunately for Celtic, so was the result because although Real had managed to pull only one goal back by the interval, they scored twice in the second half to edge Celtic out of the tournament they had won in 1967. There would be other absorbing European nights against glamorous opposition for Provan. Against Juventus in September 1981 Murdo MacLeod gave Celtic a slim lead which they could not sustain in Turin and again they lost by a single goal, this time on a 2–1 aggregate.

The following year Celtic ran up a scoreline that any team in Europe would pray for nowadays when they drew 2–2 with Ajax in Amsterdam and beat the Dutch masters with goals from Charlie Nicholas and George McCluskey to go through on a 4–3 aggregate to meet Real Sociedad, but again their progress was to be halted by Spaniards. Still, there was no reason why Provan should not look forward to further excursions in the Champions Cup, and he managed to score his single European goal in a convincing victory over Aarhus in Denmark in September 1984 in the Uefa Cup.

But he was not destined to make any more contributions to the elite tournament. Instead Provan became the victim of an illness which could not have been anticipated for the simplest of reasons – nobody had heard of it. For any career to be brought to a premature end by ill-health is poignant but when a professional sportsman or woman is stopped in their prime, it can seem as though the natural order of things has somehow been defied.

These are people for whom fitness is one of the tools of the job and whose dedication to a healthy body is a reproach to the sedentary onlooker. Footballers, though, are not insulated against certain disorders any more than the rest of us. Davie Cooper's tragic death from a massive brain haemorrhage which he suffered in the middle of a coaching session with youngsters in 1995 was a particularly tragic example but Dundalk, too, suffered a grievous loss when Liam Devine, the lad who missed the chance to knock Celtic out of the European Cup, subsequently died of cancer at a cruelly young age.

Davie Provan's career was bushwhacked by an affliction without a name or a history, although it started with a common complaint. 'I contracted the Influenza 'A' virus in the September of 1985 and I had lost about a stone in weight, which I couldn't really afford because I wasn't carrying any weight at that time, and I trained through the virus. Eventually I felt better and I put the weight back on and was playing arguably the best football I had played in years when we met Rangers in a league match at Ibrox. It was in November and I remember that Mark McGhee made his debut for Celtic after he was signed from Hamburg.

'I felt very tired that morning when I got out of bed. When the game started, within ten minutes I knew there was something seriously wrong. I remember taking a corner and I couldn't focus on the ball properly. I felt as if I had diving boots on because my legs seemed so heavy, so I told Davie Hay at half-time but when you're 2–0 down in an Old Firm game the last thing that you want to be accused of is putting up the white flag so I went out and played the second half.

'After that the problems really began. I was sleeping for 16 or 17 hours at a time and it wasn't diagnosed because it was an illness which wasn't really recognised at the time, during which period I was still being asked to turn out for the reserves. In fact, I slept in for a match, would you believe – a three o'clock kick off and I actually slept in for it.

'Eventually, I was sent to Ruchill Hospital to speak to a consultant there and within minutes of discussing the symptoms he told me I had Myalgic Encephalomyelitis and that it would probably mean that I wouldn't play again. But you don't believe doctors when they tell you that, you think you'll probably get over it. However, as time wore on I knew I wasn't getting any better and, in fact, was getting worse so that I couldn't even play four or five holes of golf which was my pastime. I went to Billy McNeill and said: look, I'm not going anywhere here.

'And he said, okay, we'll announce your retirement and he did it the day he signed Andy Walker. A testimonial match was arranged and 45,000 Celtic supporters turned up, for which I will be eternally grateful.'

The illness which had halted Provan more effectively than any bone clattering tackle had ever done is widely known now as ME but it remains a shadowy condition which can devastate its victims. It affects three times as many women as men and it is most likely to occur when the patient is aged between 30 and 40. Davie Provan was 29 when the first symptoms occurred and he retired at the age of 31.

According to the British Medical Association, the symptoms of ME are as follows:

'Fever and headache are followed by muscle pains, tenderness, weakness and severe muscle fatigue, particularly on exertion. There may also be general malaise, dizziness, nausea, numbness, and a sensation of pins-and-needles.
Psychological upset, including depression, inability to concentrate, loss of memory, sleep disturbances and panic states are common features.
The condition usually clears up completely in time, but in a few cases symptoms persist over a number of years, sometimes exacerbated by stress.'

What did not help sufferers was the label of 'Yuppie Flu' which was attached to the condition, on account of several cases being reported amongst City stockbrokers, who were suspected of being burn-out cases. It is a description which continues to offend Provan.

'It is offensive and it remains so to the ME Association because the media tagged it like that and trivialised what is a very serious illness, an illness which is wrecking people's lives now. Thankfully, most of the medical profession now accept it as an organic illness where previously so many were sceptical of its existence at all.

'Many in the medical profession considered it to be a psychological problem but it is now recognised by the mainstream medical profession, thankfully. There is an ME Association which is very well organised and is very informative and helpful to sufferers. I think I was fortunate that I was so fit at the time and so strong that perhaps I didn't get it to the extent that some people did and I managed to return to a fairly normal lifestyle, although I had to give up football.

'I would say I am now 80–90 per cent recovered but it affects other people to varying degrees and there are some tragic cases where sufferers are more or less invalids, housebound. It has taken years out of people's lives and I'm just grateful that I have been part of the process of awareness and the message that the ME Association have tried to get across to people. It is something which I have been glad to help with and which I will continue to do.'

One of the most troublesome aspects of the illness – even more so for a man used to keeping himself in peak physical condition – was the lack of any visible sign of the symptoms. Many people were sceptical that any illness truly existed and there were some doctors who openly said that it was all in the mind and that so-called sufferers were actually indulging in a con game. One of them was unwise enough to do so in Provan's presence on a TV programme which was screened throughout Britain.

'I remember being invited down to take part in the programme in London and getting involved in a very heated debate with a doctor who refused to accept that this illness did have an organic origin and he was saying that most of the people who claimed they had it were malingerers and that most of the problems associated with it were mental.

'I found his remarks deeply offensive and I made sure after the programme that I got a hold of him and explained to him that I had been forced to give up a great job, a job that I loved, that paid well, that had let me see most of the world. I said to him that there was no way this was all in my mind, tiredness and fatigue and exhaustion but unfortunately I don't think that in his case I got my message across.

'I just hope that if he had any patients who ever contracted ME that they got out of his practice and fixed up with somebody who would have a bit more understanding of it.

'It still happens, although fortunately not anything like so much, but the symptoms are so wide and varied and vague and so difficult to categorise or diagnose that it is hard for doctors to make a judgement about it. Certainly, it has left a legacy for me in that sometimes, particularly in the cold weather I don't seem to think as well as I do normally and when you're broadcasting you can't really afford to have any lapses.

'Sometimes I struggle a bit, but that apart I'm delighted at the recovery I've made and very grateful for it.'

For Provan, ME not only halted a career which would be the dream of any Celtic supporter, it also created another unpleasant legacy. Almost without exception, success at the top level of sport is achieved by individuals with a powerfully developed competitive nature – one reason why so many of them find it difficult to adjust to life after retirement. Provan was confronted with the need to find some other outlet for his competitive drive at the very time when his physical capacity was drastically reduced.

'You're dead right there,' he says, 'because there was then a competitive void and suddenly I was an onlooker at matches instead of being involved in them. I think to make it in professional football you need to have a very hard competitive edge and I eventually threw myself into golf and nowadays that's where I compete – on the golf course. Thankfully, I'm physically capable of doing so now but that was the biggest problem, not being able to compete and having to remove myself from the dressing-room environment which is such a great place to work.

'Dressing-rooms are very competitive, of course, but there is enormous empathy and bonding in a football dressing-room and I missed that so much. And having to sit and watch the team on a Saturday could be truly depressing, especially at the big games, with huge crowds and that wonderful atmosphere, knowing that I just couldn't run out there with them and that I would never do it again at an age when I should have had years of good football left in me.

'All of that involved a great deal of frustration for me because I felt that I really belonged at Celtic and that maybe if I had gone there earlier I wouldn't be quite so agitated at not being able to play for the club any more. I was 22 when I signed for Celtic because, of course, there was no freedom of contract at the time and Kilmarnock turned down four transfer requests until eventually I walked out for a few weeks. They got the message and I got the transfer to Celtic.

'When you get nine or ten years of professional football which is so enjoyable, you do have to accept that it is a remarkable privilege because it isn't the real world. It's good money for doing very little and which you enjoy in the first place. For me to actually have to try to earn a living now is a bit of an eye opener – a consequence of having had it so easy for so long.

'I think I played something like 300 games for Celtic and there are probably half a dozen matches which stand out – the Dundalk game has to be one of them for what I suppose are strange reasons. But thankfully we live in the video age now so I have a lot of the big games on tape, and now that time has passed I'm just grateful to have made some kind of contribution to the history of a great football club and to have enjoyed that empathy we had with the supporters at that time.

'It was great fun while it lasted.'

Roy Aitken

CELTIC 2 DUNDEE UNITED 1

18 May 1985

TWO memorable events happened in the Bulgarian capital of Sofia in November 1987. Scotland, who were playing out a European Championship qualifying section which was meaningless for them, beat Bulgaria 1–0 when Gary Mackay scored late in the match and guaranteed that the Republic of Ireland would reach the finals of a major tournament for the first time. So began an extraordinary ten years for the Irish team and their supporters under an English manager. For Mackay there was elevation to something like instant sainthood in bars from Cork to Donegal.

The other occurrence was played out before a rather smaller audience in the Sofia Sheraton Hotel, the first Sheraton to be built behind what was then the Iron Curtain. A few of the Scottish journalists were sitting at lunch in the restaurant when a Bulgarian waiter approached their table. The following conversation took place:

Waiter: 'Are you with the Scotland team?'

Scots: 'Yes.'

Waiter: 'Will Roy Aitken play?'

Scots: 'Yes. Why do you want to know?'

Waiter: 'Feed the bear! Feed the bear!'

At which point the waiter sprinted from the room, leaving the mystified Scots to wonder whether they had just been given a coded message by a mad MI6 agent. A few seconds later, however, the waiter returned, brandishing a copy of Aitken's autobiography – *Feed the Bear* – and in a state of high excitement, asked: 'Will he come here? Can I meet him? He can eat in this restaurant and I will serve him – I will feed the bear!'

Recognising that a picture opportunity had been handed to them on a plate so to speak, the journalists tipped off their photographers and one beatific Bulgarian waiter was duly captured with the captain of Celtic and Scotland. Exactly how a copy of *Feed the Bear* had found its way to the Sheraton Sofia was never explained but Aitken's accumulation of honours – and his reputation – had expanded steadily since he made his debut for Celtic at the age of 16 in 1975.

Not that Aitken was ever entirely enchanted with his nickname, but he made the best of it, saying: 'To be honest, I always felt that I gave everything for whatever team I was playing for and Celtic fans would know that better than any. I took it that being called the Bear was generally a complimentary remark.'

That there was a strong physical dimension to Aitken's play was never in doubt. He was, after all, sent off while playing for three different Celtic managers – Jock Stein, Billy McNeill and Davie Hay – and one of his dismissals was in the 1984 Scottish Cup final, which makes his choice of memorable game, the final of 1985, all the more significant. It was in a Scottish Cup fourth round replay against first division Kilmarnock at Rugby Park on 6 March 1977 that he was first told to make his way to the bath prematurely. Celtic lost 1–0. It was their first defeat by a lower division side since 1948.

What becomes obvious in any appraisal of Aitken's career is that whenever some large issue hung on a single game, he would usually play a crucial role in deciding the outcome. Think of the 4–2 victory over Rangers at Parkhead in 1979, when a ten-man Celtic team snatched the title in the closing minutes of one of the most enthralling Old Firm derbies ever witnessed. It was Roy Aitken's equalising goal which brought Celtic flooding back into contention.

In his 15 years with Celtic he averaged more than 44 games a season for the club, not to mention schoolboy, youth and under-21 Scottish caps which can be added to his 50 senior appearances for Scotland, and any estimate of the combative side of his nature might profitably be compared to that of Graeme Souness, another individual who responded to heightened occasions. As a Rangers player Souness was also sent off three times, against Hibernian in his first Scottish league game, against Aberdeen when Rangers won their first title in nine years and against Celtic, after a foul on Billy Stark. Souness's three red cards were shown within the space of two seasons.

Aside from which, there was an area of Aitken's game which was not always evident to spectators, but which could be discerned by managers. Jock Stein recognised it when the bear club was promoted to the first team during the spell when Stein was convalescing from the car crash which almost killed him.

'Jock asked me to come into his office,' Aitken remembers, 'and I thought that maybe he was going to tell me that I had to go back to the reserves, but he explained that he was bothered about me being asked to do too much too early. He thought that I was not just strong enough to be able to play as a central defender, although he thought it would come in good time.

'However, he didn't want me out of the side so he had decided that I should play in front of the back four where I could get forward into midfield when the chance allowed – and if I made mistakes there were still good defenders behind me who could sort it out. Funnily enough, if you look back you can see it is the same role which Scotland eventually decided suited me well.'

Andy Roxburgh, who made Aitken captain of Scotland, came back from the 1986 World Cup in Mexico, impressed by what the Brazilians called the 'magic diamond', a formation which employed four defenders and two forwards, with the midfield four deployed in a diamond shape – one player in front of the defence, one behind the attackers and two men on the flanks. Aitken would be the man in front of the back line.

To those who thought of Aitken as the rough in the diamond, Roxburgh had a ready retort. 'Roy is not the most elegant mover, it has to be said. If you were going to look for a likeness in the animal world, it would not be a gazelle which would spring to mind. But like all really good players, he thinks carefully about his game. He knows his strengths and he makes arrangements around him to limit his weaknesses. He is thoroughly reliable but he also demonstrates skills which do not get the recognition they deserve – it was Roy who made the opportunity for Gordon Strachan to score a very well worked goal against West Germany in Mexico, for example.'

When Roxburgh promoted Aitken to the captaincy of Scotland he was fulfilling a prediction made by Jock Stein. 'That boy will play for Scotland,' Stein said on his first sight of the 13-year-old boy in action. Ten years later, Stein forecast: 'He is a natural born leader who has all the makings of captain of his country.'

Versatility was always a strong suit with Aitken. Between the ages of 13 and 16 he was heavily involved with the basketball team at St Andrew's Secondary School in Saltcoats. St Andrew's won the Scottish Basketball Cup three years in a row and Aitken played for Scotland. When he was not achieving seven 'O' levels and four Highers, plus earning a certificate for proficiency at the piano ('I was daft, I stopped playing when I was 16 and I wish I hadn't,' Aitken now says), he turned out for a variety of football teams. Stamina, self-discipline and concentration – the marks of the achiever – were evident in the teenager.

Because he was an only child and probably also because his parents, John and Lily, were both working, Aitken was self-sufficient. 'I had a will to win and to succeed before I went to Celtic,' is Aitken's recollection. 'I chose to go to Celtic at a time when Ayr United were also interested because I believed they would offer me the best chance of achieving my aims and the result was that I was brought up with success. I have always made high demands of myself and a club of the calibre of Celtic insists that you should want to meet high challenges.

'I think it would be impossible for me to go through the motions at anything I tried. I put demands on myself as a player and now as a manager I put these same demands on the people who play for me. I can't remember it ever being any other way and, to be honest, I can't imagine it ever changing in that respect.'

As a boy Aitken was naturally a Celtic supporter. His father had played football for the family's local church in Ardrossan, St Peter's Star of the Sea, and had even appeared in the same team as Bobby Lennox, a distinction which was to be equalled by the son. Oddly, considering that Aitken's energies were to embrace so many sporting activities in his teenage years, he did not actually take part in an organised game of football until he was 12 years old, largely because his primary school was too small to have a team

'I think I was about ten when I first really got interested in playing and that was because my dad bought a leather ball and we went down to the park to have a kickabout. But as far as watching Celtic was concerned I didn't have a lot of time to go to games, so in that respect I wasn't an ardent fan. When football really took a grip of me I was too busy playing matches to have a chance to see many matches – not even Saltcoats Victoria. I maybe managed the odd junior game but I had to rely on television to see Celtic because most of the time I was playing every time I got a chance.'

If Aitken never saw Celtic in the flesh until he signed for the club, he swiftly made up the ground by appearing for the first team to such effect that he had captained the side by the time he was 20 and he began accumulating league and cup winners' medals at the same age. That was when Stein intervened to prevent such a fiercely burning talent from exhausting itself prematurely.

Under Billy McNeill, though, he imposed himself on two dramatic occasions.

The first was the 1979 championship win over Rangers at Celtic Park, mentioned earlier. The second was the Scottish Cup final of 1980, also against Rangers, when both the first choice Celtic centre backs, Roddie McDonald and Tom McAdam, were suspended and Aitken had to forge a makeshift partnership with Mike Conroy at the heart of the back line. The arrangement proved good enough to hold Rangers at bay and George McCluskey's deflected shot past Peter McCloy won the cup for Celtic in a game which is unfortunately better remembered for being the occasion of the Hampden Riot, an event which at least marked the end of the widespread hooliganism which used to disfigure Scottish football.

Before the 1980 final Celtic had generally been regarded as underdogs. Five years later, as they prepared to meet Dundee United in the 100th Scottish Cup final, they were favourites. Nevertheless, there was tension in the Celtic camp because the team had won nothing under Davie Hay, who had succeeded McNeill in difficult circumstances. McNeill had let it be known publicly that he thought the directors should offer him a contract – a statement which the board took to be a disguised demand for a wage rise – and he was hustled out of Celtic Park in a state of shock.

Although he was manager of Manchester City, McNeill had been invited to the 1985 final to take part in a presentation of all living captains of sides which had won the trophy and when he was introduced to the crowd, the volume and passion of cheering from the Celtic supporters was meant to convey a message to the directors about their treatment of a Parkhead legend. It could hardly fail to remind Davie Hay that he had yet to deliver anything like the stream of honours which McNeill had won as a manager.

Aitken, too, was not enjoying the unadorned approval of the fans, some of whom held him at least partially responsible for the defeat by Aberdeen the previous year, when he became the first player to be ordered off since Jock Buchanan of Rangers in 1929. Aitken has never been inclined to apologise for that contretemps, then or now.

'I did catch Mark McGhee with my hand as I went in to tackle him but it was more a piece of awkwardness than anything else. Bob Valentine of Dundee was the referee and he decided that it must have been premeditated and that I would have to go. What made me angry at the time was that before he got to me he was surrounded by Aberdeen players who were all keen to make sure he heard their version before he spoke to me.'

To make matters worse, when the game went to extra time it was McGhee who scored the goal to make it 2–1. Aitken watched from the directors' box and refused to take part in the presentation of the losers' medals and eventually received his unwanted souvenir from Mark Reid, who collected it on his behalf. In the dressing-room Hay told Aitken that something would have to give – either a positional change was required . . . or a new club. To add to the day's delights, McGhee won the Mr Superfit award, presented by the match sponsors to the fittest man on the field.

Lesser players would have taken shelter from the inevitable fallout, but not Aitken, who that evening fulfilled a commitment to attend a Celtic supporters' club function in Coatbridge, at which he was well received. Between times, though, a Skol Cup final was lost to Rangers – another game which saw Celtic deprived of a prize in extra time – when Ally McCoist scored from a penalty kick awarded after Aitken had fouled him in the box.

So the approach to the 1985 final was lined with hazard warning lights for Aitken, although at Celtic's last press conference before the match he insisted that the events of the previous year had only sharpened his desire to return to the scene of his misfortunes and that the final would bring together the two best footballing sides in Scotland.

'Although Aberdeen have scored more goals than any other side, I think Dundee United and Celtic are the most attack-minded teams in the league. We both play two wide players and use a similar formation and we are not afraid to have a go. But although United have a lot of good players, ours are better. If we play on the day we will win. It's two years since we won anything and for a club like this that's long enough.'

Aitken added that he expected the game to yield goals but Eamonn Bannon, the United midfielder, disagreed and said that a free-scoring contest would result only if someone scored early. 'I simply can't see it happening,' Bannon said. 'Both teams are likely to play it very tight from the start because the first 20 minutes of any match, far less a cup final, are vital.'

There was an unwelcome distraction for Celtic three days before the final when Mo Johnston was found guilty at Glasgow District Court of reselling three track suits worth a total of £85 in July 1983, when he was with Partick Thistle, and was fined £200. Stipendiary Magistrate Robert Hamilton told the abashed forward: 'I could really make a name for myself and lock you up and perhaps get the freedom of Dundee on Saturday.' Certainly, Johnston was not about to be given the freedom of the Dundee United defence at Hampden.

Two days before the match Celtic retreated to their usual big event base at Seamill Hydro on the Firth of Clyde. The build-up went according to plan until the Friday when, in a bizarre turn of events, Aitken was almost ruled out of contention. 'A few of us went down to visit my friend Mark Reid and have a cup of tea. I bent down to pick up my cup and felt a little jerk in my back. It didn't seem anything at the time but the longer the day went on after that, the more my back began to tighten up. Obviously there had been a muscle spasm or maybe a tweaked nerve – if it had been a tear I would have had no chance of playing the next day – but I crawled to my bed that evening, literally crawled, and thought that I was out of it all.

'But I got up the next morning and felt a little easier, took some muscle relaxants which helped so that I was able to take a fitness test. I was taken up to Glasgow in a car, to a specialist called George Abrami in Carmunnock. He looked at it, gave me pain killers and basically told me to get on with it. So what began as a very serious problem didn't hold me back in the end but it was very alarming and it was the most anxious morning I've spent before a cup final,' is Aitken's recollection.

'Even so, my whole attention was focused on the game and making sure that if was declared fit I would be properly ready to play. Certainly, the build-up was a bit different but once George Abrami had cleared me I was able to get off to meet up with the team bus just outside Glasgow and settle back into the usual routine. As you would expect, I was very relieved to know I was playing, not only because it was an important game but because of what had happened the previous year.

'It wasn't so much having been sent off, albeit that I felt that it had been unjust, and it was not a pleasant experience but by a year later I regarded it as water under the bridge. It was that I believed very strongly that having lost in the previous final it was vital that we should follow a defeat of the previous season with a victory, because that is the Celtic way.

'Danny McGrain was the captain that day but I always liked to take a bit of responsibility because I felt it was part and parcel of my role to try to bring out the best in other players. I did go round and speak to most people but I also had to make sure I was exactly right to take part, which meant getting a couple of extra rubs in the dressing-room.

'I wasn't the superstitious type and I didn't have any specific routine that I went through, unlike the boys who wanted to go out first or last or put one certain boot on before the other. What I did like was to get out on the pitch well before the game started. Again that isn't something that every player enjoys but for me it was always a good thing to do, especially on an occasion like the cup final when the atmosphere builds all the time and you can start to become involved in it. I loved to get a feel of the razzamatazz, the excitement, the crowds coming in and starting their singing and the bands playing away on the pitch.'

It was evident soon after referee Brian McGinlay had set the proceedings in motion that Eamonn Bannon was more likely to be accurate in his forecast than Aitken. Dundee United were the masters in Scotland of absorbing pressure almost willingly and then breaking on the counter-attack after their opponents had been sucked too far upfield. So it proved on this occasion.

The following morning *Sunday Mail* readers were told by Allan Herron: 'United had brilliantly blunted and frustrated the Celtic attacking system throughout so much of the game. Dave Narey snuffed out the forays of Mo Johnston and Paul Hegarty made Frank McGarvey's life a misery in this 100th final. Celtic simply carried no danger despite the Herculean attempts of their power man, Roy Aitken, to organise the men around him.

'When Stuart Beedie scored for United, when they were flowing with precision in the 54th minute, frankly it looked all over.'

Bannon was instrumental in creating the opportunity, laying off a pass to Davie Dodds on the left side of the box with Aitken in an awkward tackling position. Dodds shielded the ball and turned it ahead of Beedie who drove it low past Bonner in the Celtic goal. The United fans had been subdued in comparison with their Celtic counterparts but now the Tannadice support was cavorting in a tangerine and black frolic on their terracings and Celtic looked weary as it rained unremittingly.

United were not the kind of side who would recklessly press on in pursuit of another goal to put the game out of Celtic's reach, and they frequently seemed content to let Hay's players have possession 30 or 40 yards out secure in the knowledge that the defence in front of Hamish McAlpine was notoriously difficult to break down. Bannon remarked years later, after he had left Tannadice to join Hearts, that it was only when he played against United that he had realised what a defensively minded team they were.

'They definitely sat on their lead,' Aitken recalls. 'That was an art which they had perfected both at domestic and European level. Yet there was not a point in that game where I felt we were looking at a lost cause, probably because they were fairly happy to let us come at them and I knew that we were not in much danger of conceding another goal. In that Celtic team there was a very strong spririt and we had players who could be relied upon to fight until the last kick of the ball.'

Even so, both sets of supporters sensed that fighting spirit alone would not dislodge United's stubborn defenders and that something more inspired would be necessary. With the game about to move into its final quarter hour, Hay gambled. He withdrew Paul McStay and replaced him with Pierce O'Leary, who moved into the centre of the Celtic defence, freeing Aitken to push into midfield. Aitken's back had begun to stiffen but it was he who stiffened the back of a Celtic side which desperately required a sense of urgency. The Bear had ueen set loose in the middle of the park and he began clawing at the ramparts around the United penalty area.

Within two minutes of the tactical switch, the gamble paid and Celtic drew level. Murdo MacLeod was foraging around the edge of the United box, probing for an opening in the tightly grouped tangerine ranks when he was caught from behind by none other than Eamonn Bannon. It was a clear free kick in an extremely hazardous position for U~ 'ted and Celtic disguised their intentions to excellent effect.

Davie Provan, master of the exquisitely flighted ball, was on hand along with MacLeod, who could strike a venomous shot, as Brian McGinlay checked that the United defensive wall would keep its ten-yard distance. Provan took the kick and with utter command of trajectory he curled the ball over the wall and just under the crossbar beyond the reach of the clawing McAlpine. In that moment the shape of the game was reversed. Now it was United whose players looked perplexed and whose fans had fallen silent. Now it was Celtic who had banished fatigue and who were lifted by the bedlam from their supporters, particularly the vast congregation massed behind McAlpine's goal.

'We were shooting into the traditional Celtic end and that in itself becomes a force because every time you move on to the attack you can hear them roar and see that huge mass of green and white and you actually feel them sucking you towards the goal. It also has the effect on the opposition of making them defend deeper and deeper and after we got the equaliser it was like the Alamo because we were going at them in waves and it was just a matter of time before we broke through again.

'I think it's natural that when you are one up, as United were, and then lose a goal like that, something gives inside you because you then have to begin all over and lift it again. Once you've set your stall out to defend a lead which you think can take you to full-time it's so much harder to go back on to the offensive again.

'I felt very strongly that we wouldn't have to go to extra time because before we got the winning goal we had made one or two good chances and that just fired the crowd up even more, so the atmopshere increasingly favoured us and was not helping them. United were reeling a little bit, which encouraged us to push harder and harder at them.'

United were indeed buckling and when they were caught on the back foot too close to their own goal six minutes from the end, it was Aitken who fashioned the winning strike. 'I played a header forward and Paul Hegarty headed it back into my path. When it came back to me I decided I would take a touch to my right and I hit a hard cross into an area where I knew my forwards would be. Frank McGarvey threw himself at it and his header went in from about ten yards.

'Frank has always claimed it as his goal but I said at the time that it was really a one-two by me off Frank. Anyway, off went Frank in his own individual style to celebrate behind the goal with our supporters. I saw him go over to the fans and the next thing I knew, Frank had fallen in a heap. The story he gave us later was that he had actually fainted for a couple of seconds. Typical McGarvey.'

If McGarvey did keel over in the emotion of the moment he was in good company. United had been flattened as well. Still, they could not be dicounted in the closing moments as both sides adapted to another psychological shift.

'Once we went 2–1 ahead our game plan then changed a little bit in the sense that we said to ourselves, right, the main job now is to make sure that we don't lose this, so the other team is almost guaranteed a last chance. In their case it was a half chance with Pierce O'Leary knocking the ball away from the head of Paul Sturrock just a couple of minutes before the end with a scissors kick out of the box.

'By that time I didn't feel we were in any danger of losing because no matter what had happened in the rest of the game, in the space of something like ten to 15 minutes we had annihilated Dundee United and I couldn't see how they had anything else to give which was really going to cause us any problems.'

As Allan Herron put it in the *Sunday Mail* next morning: 'Six minutes from time this unstoppable force called Aitken hit a difficult cross from the right against the retreating Tayside defence and for once McGarvey was in the right place at the right time. We had witnessed a truly tremendous effort from a team that looked dead and buried in a sensational second half. No doubt about the man of the match – it was Aitken, determined to make amends in this final after being ordered off last season.

'I've never seen one player give so much in one game and change the pattern of any final. One has to feel sorry for Jim McLean and his players. The trophy they have never won eluded them and yet they did so much correctly. They appeared to carry more danger than Celtic because they were better at moving the ball about and controlled the play, but in the end it was all about passion and aggression.

'And Aitken showed all of that.'

Jim Reynolds, writing in the *Glasgow Herald* two days after the game, focused on the transformation which overtook both sides after Celtic had drawn level: 'United's heads went down and Celtic moved up a gear as they sensed the cup was theirs for the taking. With just six minutes left they grabbed a stunning winner and it was appropriate that Aitken should have set it up. He galloped down the right, shrugged off a challenger and swung the cross over. McGarvey threw himself forward and scored with a diving header – a goal fit to win any match.'

There was barely any chance for Aitken to savour his part in the triumph. After the match Celtic made their way to the Grosvenor Hotel in Glasgow's West End for a victory dinner which was celebrated in marked contrast to their depressed gathering at the same venue 12 months previously. After an evening's dancing with his wife Jane and the rest of the squad and spouses, Aitken had to join the Scotland squad assembling to prepare for a Rous Cup match against England at Hampden Park on the following Saturday and a World Cup qualifying tie with Iceland in Reykyavik ten days later.

Both matches ended in single goal wins for the Scots, courtesy of a header from Richard Gough at Hampden and a Jim Bett penalty kick in Iceland and Aitken was at last free to reflect upon a season which had come good for him in its final days.

What struck him most ironically when he looked at his newly expanded collection of honours was the bonus shield he collected after the final. Aitken, the man who had almost missed the chance to pick up the Scottish Cup because he had bent down to pick up a teacup, was the sponsors' choice . . . as Mr Superfit.

Murdo MacLeod

RANGERS 4 CELTIC 4

22 March 1986

TO read the history of Old Firm games is to risk an overdose of superlatives – not all of them deserved. The endless passion of both sets of supporters for these fixtures sometimes overpowers the football on offer and just as frequently transforms what would, in other circumstances, be an unremarkable contest into something which can sound as though it involved a collision of the Viking gods.

From time to time, though, a football match has consequences which go far beyond any reckoning which could reasonably have been made beforehand, although it is important to remember the distinction to be made between the game itself and the circumstances which attend it. For example, the disasters at Ibrox (1972), the Heysel Stadium (1985) and at Hillsborough (1989) came about because of failures of crowd control.

On the pitch there are games such as Celtic's European Cup win of 1967 which herald some great shift in the sport's balance of power. In the 11 years prior to the Lisbon Lions' triumph no team outside Italy, Portugal or Spain had ever won the trophy; after Celtic beat Inter Milan the Cup only left northern Europe once in the next 18 years.

Another game which can be argued to have transformed Scottish football – although nobody could have foreseen that at the time – took place on 22 March 1986, when Rangers met Celtic in the final Old Firm derby of that season, a contest which has remained particularly vivid in the memory of all who saw it or played in it. It was a game whose subsequent impact on both clubs would have seemed the stuff of utter fantansy at the time. How else was it likely to be when the match was a fixture in which the fourth team in the premier division played the fifth side in the table? For once the Glasgow rivarly was overshadowed by Edinburgh's derby because at Easter Road Hibernian were at home to a Hearts team which was 21 games into an extraordinary unbeaten run which had started before Christmas and which propelled them into the league leadership.

In the event, Hearts were to sustain that position until seven minutes from the end of their final game away to Dundee at Dens Park when the first of Albert Kidd's two goals for the home side allowed Celtic – who had barnstormed their way to a 5–0 lead over St Mirren at Love Street – to edge ahead on goal difference and snatch the title in unlikely circumstances. But again, that was not a prospect which seemed at all likely as Celtic made their way to Ibrox on a day of torrential spring rains for a derby which offered Davie Hay's players an opportunity to wipe out the memory of a 3–0 defeat on their previous visit in November.

Not only were Hearts top of the league but there were formidable obstacles immediately behind them in the shapes of Dundee United and Aberdeen, both of whom fancied themselves for the championship. Unusually on the occasion of an Old Firm derby, most of the top sportswriters had made their way to Edinburgh for a game which looked much more significant than the meeting of two mid-table sides at Ibrox. And their choice seemed justified when, at the end of the afternoon, Celtic and Rangers had both lost ground to Hearts, who finished 2–1 winners over Hibs.

In fact, the table showed Hearts on 41 points followed by Dundee United (38), Aberdeen (36), Celtic (34) and Rangers (32), and although Davie Hay and his team had games in hand they were running short of time to make an impact on the championship race. It was already accepted that Rangers were out of the running and their most serious concern was being overtaken by Dundee, only one point behind, in the chase for the last available place in the Uefa Cup.

It had been a miserable season for Rangers all round. They had been ditched from the Skol Cup by Hibs in the semi-finals and from the Scottish Cup by Hearts in the third round. Not that Celtic were much better off – Hibs had knocked them out of the Skol Cup in a penalty kick decider after a 4–4 draw in the quarter-finals and at the same stage of the Scottish Cup the Edinburgh team again won a high scoring encounter, 4–3 this time.

So the Old Firm derby, as usual, provided one measure of health for each set of supporters, the chance to boast that no matter how their star might have faded in the football universe at least their team was still superior to the other lot. Rangers had already been in such a morose position and it was their 3–0 victory over Celtic in November which offered them a flicker of hope of improvement amidst defeats by Dundee (twice), Aberdeen, Hibs, St Mirren and Hearts. However, on 15 March Dundee had inflicted yet another reverse on them with a 2–1 win at Dens Park.

As he took the field a couple of minutes before kick-off, Murdo MacLeod reflected, not for the first time, that if Rangers had taken any of their chances to sign him, he would probably now be walking out in a light blue jersey rather than the Hoops. Not that he had been a Rangers supporter as a boy. Murdo, whose powerful running from midfield allied with a venomous shot and resolute tackling, had earned him the nickname of 'Rhino' from the Celtic fans, came from a footballing family of diverse loyalties.

His father, also called Murdo, played for Hibs – and is not to be confused with John Murdoch MacLeod, another Easter Road star of similar vintage – at inside right. MacLeod senior also played for Maryhill Juniors as well as Cumnock, reaching the Scottish Junior Cup final with the Ayrshire side. Alistair, brother of Murdo (junior), was a footballer too and plied his trade with Dumbarton and Kilmarnock as well as Raith Rovers.

'With that background I was much more interested in playing football when I was a boy than supporting anybody,' MacLeod was to recollect when his own career in the game had fetched him up at Firhill, where he succeeded John Lambie as manager of Partick Thistle in August 1995. 'I supported the team I was playing for, whoever they might be.

'People say to me, "Ach, ye're talkin' nonsense," but since I was about seven or eight years old I was playing for the 2nd Milngavie Junior BB, I was playing in school teams and then Partick Thistle Boys Club between under-13 and under-15 and Glasgow Amateurs. I was so busy playing, sometimes four or five times a week that I never, ever saw a lot of football when I was young. It was when I had signed for Glasgow Amateurs that the senior clubs began to watch and ask if I would come and play trials for them.

'At the time, I was training at Ibrox, I'd been to Arsenal, Crystal Palace, Wolves. I was also training at Boghead and it might seem strange for some people to understand why I chose Dumbarton but it was because Alex Wright, who was the manager at the time, said to me that if I joined Dumbarton I would get my chance earlier than I would at other clubs. It was a case of, if you're good enough with us you'll get to the big clubs anyway, but if you go there first you could get lost amongst 30 or 40 kids.

'I had the chance to sign for Rangers when I was leaving school at 16 and I had another opportunity to go to Ibrox when it was time for leaving Dumbarton. Rangers were looking at me at the time but so were Celtic. In the end, it was Celtic who came in first with the bid and so I was honoured to sign for them. I think when you're with Celtic, it's such an institution that your thoughts are turned entirely towards it.

'Even now, I still have an awful lot of feeling for the club, which is not surprising, I suppose, because I played 360 games for Celtic. But as I say, I was the kind of person who devoted myself to whoever I was playing for at the time and I still have strong feelings about Borussia Dortmund – I played 150 games for them – and Hibernian because I played a hundred games for them. I believed when I was a player that the club is entitled to your absolute commitment and I haven't changed my views in any way since I've been a manager.'

MacLeod was to be linked with a move to Rangers – or rather, Rangers let it be known that they would certainly be interested if he chose not to renew his contract with Celtic in 1983 – but in one of his last acts as manager, Billy McNeill made sure that the club would retain a particularly valued asset. It was a time when the club badly needed to stand its ground in the face of challenges from unexpected quarters. In 1982–83 Dundee United had become champions for the first time in the Tannadice club's history despite a surge by Celtic on the final day of the season.

Dundee United beat Dundee 2–1 at Dens Park to secure the title on the last afternoon of the season, while Celtic beat Rangers 4–2 at Ibrox. Had United drawn 1–1 then Celtic's win would have brought them exactly even with United on points and goal difference, with the same goals for and against totals – a dead heat. For the next two years Aberdeen were champions as the so-called New Firm of the north-east of Scotland became dominant at the expense of the Glasgow clubs.

The traditional power base of the Old Firm was further eroded when Alex MacDonald's Hearts started their long undefeated run and as winter gave way to spring with no evidence that the

Tynecastle team were about to be stopped, it became increasingly probable that the title would go to an east coast club for the fourth season in succession.

'Hearts first went to the top of the league when Scotland were travelling to Australia to play off for the final place in the World Cup finals in Mexico and they were able to get games in at that time because they didn't have players in the squad,' MacLeod recollects. 'So at first, the other clubs below them had games in hand and it was more or less assumed that they would all catch up. But it didn't work out like that because Hearts went on a fabulous roll and we didn't get the opportunity to play our extra games, so not only was there a gap but Hearts kept on extending their lead.

'After a while there was a change in the way everyone began to look at the situation because with a dozen games to go people started asking who could catch Hearts. Then with half a dozen games to go, they were relentless, and the only way they would be caught was if we could take them right to the final game of the season. That looked more and more difficult because Hearts had taken the points and we had still to get them by winning our games. We knew when we went to Ibrox that if we lost that game we probably wouldn't be able to make up the ground.'

The early stages of the match were typical of the Old Firm – typical, but not classic, because with both sides nervy about a season which might leave them unacceptably barren of any achievements, the tension in the air was more palpable than usual, even for the customarily superheated climate of a Glasgow derby. The unending downpour did not help, with the ball skimming off the surface here or holding up on the wet grass there, and players unable to control their movements fully at pace on a greasy top.

Both managers selected starting line-ups which surprised their supporters. Jock Wallace kept Davie Cooper – who was in line for a place in Alex Ferguson's squad for Mexico '86 – on the bench. Davie Hay similarly chose to hold back Alan McInally, on an afternoon which might have been thought ideal for a forceful centre forward. Peter Grant was also named as a substitute.

Driven by 32,500 of their supporters in a crowd of 41,006 – it says something for the respective standings of the sides that not even an Old Firm derby at that stage could guarantee a capacity audience – Rangers carried the contest to Celtic throughout the opening period and Willie McStay was booked after quarter of an hour for a foul on Ted McMinn. Although Celtic looked to be on the back foot they accomplished the reversal of fortune which is such a characteristic of Glasgow derbies and scored with their first real goalmouth chance.

Paul McStay started the move in central midfield by sweeping the ball away to the left where Owen Archdeacon was stationed and he struck a low cross which was helped on by MacLeod into the path of Mo Johnston who took it first time from eight yards and struck it low past Nicky Walker. Rangers were knocked out of their stride by this setback and some of the challenges became confrontational. Ted McMinn, who was by now involved in something of a feud with Willie McStay, was shown the yellow card for fouling the Celtic full back and McStay twisted the knife by taking the free kick himself.

Just as his brother had done a few minutes earlier, Willie picked out Archdeacon and again the young winger set up a scoring chance, this time with a low cross which Brian McClair met with a left-foot drive to beat Walker. With the Celtic support outshouting the silent majority of Rangers supporters, the pendulum abruptly swung away from Davie Hay's players almost at the very moment when they appeared to be comfortably in control. Willie McStay was ordered off by referee David Syme for another illegal challenge on McMinn on the touchline and before Celtic could reorganise they had conceded a goal when Ian Durrant released Ally McCoist on the left for a cross which swung towards the back post where Cammy Fraser headed past Packie Bonner from six yards.

'We had played in a few Old Firm games in that period where the pattern was that one side would be playing well from the beginning and then find themselves a goal or two down,' MacLeod says. 'In this game in particular they started very well but couldn't get themselves ahead. Then we went up the park and scored which was the signal for us to start dominating the game and when we got the second we hardly had time to think that we should keep hold of it for a wee while because we were suddenly down to ten men when Willie got himself sent off.

'The rain never stopped pouring and I think that was one of the reasons for Willie getting the red card. He was sliding into tackles and maybe just pushing them a little bit quicker into Ted McMinn. The ball was skiting across the grass but it wasn't a dirty game. I think the only confrontation was between Willie and Ted, both of them having been booked, and I remember that it was at the Celtic end 15 yards up the touchline with McMinn chasing a ball and keeping it in right on the line.

'Willie was chasing after him, obviously thinking he could get to the ball but by the time McMinn turned and nicked the ball away Willie was arriving. He caught Ted late and because he had been booked earlier he really had to be sent off. So we were down to ten men but that Celtic side definitely had a fighting quality to it and we always thought we could beat anybody, even if we were a man short. Sure, it was backs to the wall but at no point were we feeling sorry for ourselves and thinking, oh, we're going to lose this.

'Even though Rangers were bringing themselves back into the game, as you would expect from the losing side in any Old Firm game, we thought we would just go on much as before until we had got the winner, whenever that might be.'

There were a couple more yellow cards before half-time with Mo Johnston and Hugh Burns, Rangers' right back, squaring up to each other on the touchline. At the interval the two managers decided on substitutions. Mindful of the likelihood that Celtic would tire towards the end of the game, Davie Hay withdrew an attacker, Archdeacon, and replaced him with Peter Grant. Jock Wallace, aware that it would not take much to inflame McMinn into some rashness that would merit a red card, left him out for the second half and threw on Davie Cooper.

Before the two formations could settle into their new patterns Celtic went two goals ahead for the second time in the game. Only two minutes into the half Johnston, who had dropped off the attack momentarily, threaded a beautifully judged pass through the Rangers back line and into the path of Tommy Burns, who strode on to draw Walker and beat the goalkeeper with a low left-foot drive from 14 yards. Celtic were now shooting towards their own supporters, who were in a ferment of disbelieving celebration.

But there was much, much more unlikely drama yet to be played out and the Celtic fans were allowed a mere five minutes to orchestrate their choral singing before they were silenced by Ally McCoist, who ran hard at the centre of the Celtic defence and from the edge of the box kept his head over the ball to thrash a powerful low strike beyond Bonner. Seven minutes down the line the sides were level and this time it was Robert Fleck who scored for Rangers, with the help of a degree of good fortune. His first attempt was a miskick but he got the break of a rebound from a Celtic boot and he hit his second effort well, high into the net.

It was the Rangers supporters' turn to party as three sides of the ground seethed with blue scarves and banners. Four minutes later they took the lead for the first time in the contest in circumstances of considerable personal interest to Murdo MacLeod, not that he was about to advertise the fact.

'That's right – I remember the goal fairly well because it was a funny sort of score by Dave McKinnon. He got a reasonable header in from about 16 yards but it was a big looping one which dropped towards our back post where a lot of players on both sides were jumping either to try and clear it or to head it on into the net, but all of them missed it completely and the ball just dropped into our net.

'So that was them in front and with the goal being scored at the Rangers end it was complete bedlam, their supporters yelling and dancing all around us. Now I used to have a wee chat with some of their players if the ball was dead for a while – although obviously not if they'd just scored – but this goal was a bit awkward because Davie McKinnon is a second cousin of mine and we used to enjoy a bit of crack during a game, especially that game.

'He came over to tell me about his goal. He said to me: 'It's usually you who scores in Old Firm games, but what about that for a goal?' He was really chuffed with himself because I think that was his first goal in an Old Firm game. One or two of the other Rangers players were claiming it – Cammy Fraser and Robert Fleck were both shouting that they had got a touch on the way in – but he told me in no uncertain terms that it was his goal and nobody else's.

'The cameras proved that it was his goal, incidentally. But you always get the last laugh if you score afterwards and that's what happened because, as I said, we were never the kind of side that would assume we were going to lose a game even if we fell behind. We just got on with it again and battled against everything until it started to go our way.

'When we did get the equaliser I scored it with the kind of shot that had become a bit of a trademark with me. I used to get a good few from outside the box and in this case the ball was just rolling inside towards me. I should know who gave it to me because I've watched it often enough on video but I would be telling a lie if I said a name. Anyway, when I saw the ball coming up at me it wasn't one of these situations where you think, well, I'm 25 yards from goal, the keeper's coming out, there are three Rangers players in front of me so I'm going to do this clever thing.

'It was just Murdo MacLeod's style at the time, take a ball, take a good touch and get a proper strike on it. As it happens, it was against the man who is my goalkeeper now at Partick Thistle, Nicky Walker, so maybe he had a wee vision of what was to come and thought, I'll just let this one go past me and keep a gaffer happy for the future.

'But it was a good strike, a very good strike. I managed a few of those against Rangers and that one was as good as any of them. Plus the fact I hit the net right in front of our own supporters and it's quite amazing how many of them I have met years later – I still meet them – and they can tell me what seat they were sitting in and how they saw it going in. Mostly it's a case of "Oh Murdo, I was right in direct line with the ball" so there must have been about six thousand people at the Celtic end with the ball coming straight at them.

'From my end it wasn't bad either. It looked all right to me and I was so busy celebrating that I forgot to have a wee word with Davie McKinnon.'

Even then, there might have been one further staggering turn of events because with Celtic tiring in the last few minutes – Packie Bonner was booked for time wasting when he kicked the ball away – Fleck set up an outstanding chance for McCoist but for once the Rangers striker would not get the benefit of an easy goal because Bonner hurled himself across the line of the shot and blocked it from no more than two yards.

And so Old Firm pride was satisfied on both sides. There would be no gloating at work or school on Monday morning by one set of euphoric partisans and no surreptitious mutterings from their depressed opposite numbers. For once both teams left the field to the ear-throbbing acclaim of every spectator in the stadium.

'That is something which will stick in my mind forever,' MacLeod says. 'All round the ground they were singing and cheering and dancing. It's very rare that everybody goes away from an Old Firm match happy with what they saw but that was one of the odd occasions when it did happen and it was a quite fantastic sight, especially for the players in the middle of it all, looking everywhere and seeing nothing but people applauding their team. If somebody had been dropped into Ibrox who didn't know which game was being played they would have thought that here were two teams who had just won the European Cup at the same time.'

For MacLeod, it had been an outstanding example of a fixture which he savoured throughout his time at Celtic Park. 'Aye, I loved playing in the Celtic-Rangers games. They're possibly the best games ever to be involved with, although maybe the reason I thoroughly enjoyed them was that I was lucky enough to have scored a lot of goals in Old Firm derbies and the goals I got were usually winners or equalisers.

'The first time I scored against Rangers was in the 4-2 game at Celtic Park in 1979, which was our last match of the season and we had to win to take the title. We were down to the last kick of the ball near enough and I scored the sixth goal in that. I got the eighth goal in the 4–4 match and I scored the winner against Rangers in the League Cup final in '82–'83. It got to be a bit of a habit, really.'

For all MacLeod's enthusiasm about the Glasgow rivalry, his awareness of the wider football world allows him to put Celtic and Rangers into perspective. He left Celtic in 1987 to move to the German Bundesliga club Borussia Dortmund, where his unvarnished style swiftly endeared him to the supporters. Foreigners often perceive the Germans as a reserved people, wary of displaying much emotion in front of strangers but to visit Borussia Dortmund in MacLeod's company is to experience at first hand how demonstrative, good-humoured and hospitable they can be when relaxed.

The directors' lounge at the Westfalen Stadion is a handsome wood-panelled room where steins of foaming lager are readily pulled for the visitor and McLeod's entrance is saluted by vigorous shouts of 'Murdo! Wilkommen!' Bearing in mind that when Borussia moved from their old ground – the Rote Erde Kampfbahn – in 1970, excavations at the Westfalen Stadion site uncovered a grand total of 34 unexploded British bombs from World War II, it may seem incongruous that the Dortmund support should take so readily to a British incomer.

However, the Westfalen Stadion was voted the country's most popular ground in a survey of German players, who thought its atmosphere was 'typisch Englisch'. The supporters are known for the 'Dortmund Roar' and to hear it in full cry is to be reminded of the intensity of Glasgow's football loyalties rather than the average English club support.

'I think on two or three occasions during my spell there the atmosphere did come up to the level you would expect from an Old Firm game, because the Dortmund supporters weren't typical of German crowds. They were there to really get behind the team, rather than watch a game as most Germans tend to do, and I think it would be unfair to suggest that Dortmund fans couldn't be as noisy as Celtic or Rangers supporters when they wanted to be,' is MacLeod's verdict.

'We played Schalke 04, which is the local equivalent of Celtic v. Rangers and every time we came up against Schalke it was sold out for weeks beforehand, even when we played at Schalke where they can hold 70,000 supporters – no chance of a ticket if you hadn't bought one weeks ahead of the game. So in that respect it was similar to an Old Firm derby and the noise wouldn't be far off the mark either, although the fans were singing for different reasons, of course. In Germany – and anywhere else if it comes to that – a derby is a purely local matter, nothing else, whereas Celtic and Rangers, Glasgow, the religious thing, makes it unique and that's what keeps Old Firm games pretty much the same no matter how the two teams might be doing.

'You find with certain clubs – Celtic and Rangers in Scotland, Manchester United, Liverpool, Newcastle in England – that the fans are very closely linked with the club, a lot more so than most other supporters are with their teams and in Germany that was the case with Borussia Dortmund, which was something that helped me settle very quickly.

'My style of play was what they wanted in a footballer. I was a winner one hundred per cent, I ran, I battled. The Germans loved that and Dortmund is a working-class city with supporters who put their backs into their jobs and who like to play hard, too. They would pay their last five or six marks to go and watch the team, similar to what people do here in Glasgow. So I was lucky that I fitted in very well over there because once I had been in Germany a while I realised that there were other clubs, some of them big name outfits, where I wouldn't have done so well.

'Of course, being west of Scotland people we think Celtic v. Rangers is world famous, which it is up to a point. But although most German supporters would probably have heard of it, they're a bit vague about the details. I used to have them coming to me and asking which was the Protestant team and which was the Catholic team, what was it all about and why did religion come into it? They couldn't see why this was such a passionate game because of religion and not just because the teams were rivals in the same city. It's not very easy to explain to foreigners.

'We're passionate in our own way but other countries have their own passions. You and I have been at Genoa v. Sampdoria where the ground was more or less full two hours before the kick-off and there was plenty of racket from both sets of fans. Same with Inter v. AC Milan. I played in a game in Turkey – and most people here wouldn't believe this – but the ground was full at nine o'clock in the morning and the kick-off wasn't until three in the afternoon. Mind you the weather's a wee bit warmer in Turkey.

'For me, the thing that makes any derby game special is the feeling for everybody involved in it that their game is the most important in the world, at least for that 90 minutes. I suppose that's because when people live next to each other and support two different clubs, they're always arguing with each other about who's better than who and if your team wins the derby, you've won the argument for another few months.

'I think Old Firm games will always have quite a turbulent atmosphere although whether it will be as strong as it has been in the past is another matter. The two clubs have done a lot to get away from the sectarian image and it will take time to tell if that will calm the atmosphere down at all. On the other hand, I think the atmosphere is the attraction of that fixture for most of the crowd and I would imagine that if there is one hundred per cent commitment from the players then there will be one hundred per cent backing from the crowds

'The history of Celtic and Rangers and the way so many people get themselves worked up about who is on top means that there is this strong tendency to see only that particular game and forget sometimes that there is a lot of football being played elsewhere. There have always been people who follow the Old Firm who are only concerned with those two teams and who couldn't care less – or don't even know – what goes on elsewhere.'

Which brings us back to the Old Firm derby played to an eight-goal draw on that March afternoon in 1986. It was hailed as a phenomenal occasion by the reporters who did witness it. The Saturday Pink edition of the *Evening Times* set the tone. Underneath its headline – OLD FIRM'S FIREWORKS – Alan Davidson wrote: 'The honours were shared as Rangers and Celtic turned in one of the most exciting – and amazing contests in history.'

Chick Young added: 'The action matched the weather at sodden Ibrox. The key word was stormy. I don't think I can recall a match between the Big Two which was in this class for excitement and drama and I certainly won't forget this one.'

MacLeod travelled down to Turnberry next morning to link up with the Scotland players from whom the 1986 World Cup finals squad would be drawn. 'I got to Turnberry, where we were all to undergo fitness tests and medical checks and the main topic of conversation was our game the day before. Walter Smith, who was at Dundee United at the time, said that he couldn't believe it had happened. He kept going on about how it should never have been possible for a team to let in four goals in an Old Firm game and certainly not for a side to score four goals and not win the match.

'But after Walter had seen it on television he came to me and said: "Well I can believe it now but you had to see it happen." I said to him that it was still hard to believe it and I had scored.'

There was, however, one man who had watched the proceedings at Ibrox and who took exactly the same view as Walter Smith. David Holmes, the chairman of Rangers, was arriving at the conclusion that Jock Wallace, for all his previous successes as manager, could not revitalise a club which was losing its way in Scottish football and which was being surpassed by Aberdeen, Dundee United, Hearts and, of course, Celtic.

A week later, on 29 March, Hearts consolidated their lead in the premier division when they beat Rangers 3–1 at Tynecastle. The next weekend was blank for the Ibrox club because of their Scottish Cup exit. To fill the gap they arranged a friendly with Tottenham Hotspur. Dismal Rangers were jeered from the field by the supporters who had bothered to turn out in a meagre crowd.

On Monday, 6 April, Jock Wallace resigned after a discussion with Holmes who had, in fact, already appointed Graeme Souness as manager. The revolution which would shake Scottish football from its outmoded, complacent ways, had begun. With hindsight the progression of events which followed Souness's appointment seems so natural that it is hard to imagine that there might have been any alternative.

But there is scope to play the tantalising game of What If. Had Rangers lost to a depleted Celtic side in that final derby of the 1985–86 season then in all likelihood Wallace would have been gone by the following Monday. The 4–4 draw gave him a fractional breathing space until Hearts and Tottenham Hotspur administered the *coup de grâce*. Suppose, though, Rangers had beaten Celtic and, buoyed by renewed confidence, had gone on a roll until the end of the season, allowing Wallace to make a case for cash to spend on buying three or four players during the summer.

Celtic might still have won the championship on the climactic final afternoon (assuming that Rangers had taken at least a point from Hearts at Tynecastle) but is it too much to imagine a revitalised challenge from Ibrox the following season? Sceptics might care to remember the case of Everton who had won the Cup Winners Cup in Rotterdam a year earlier. Fifteen months before that triumph the outlook had looked bleak for their manager, Howard Kendall.

The first two weeks of January, 1984 saw tabloid headlines devoted to predictions that the Goodison Park directors would bow to the 'Kendall Out!' chants of their supporters and find a more charismatic replacement. They dropped to 18th in the league, their worst position for four years, and on 18 January Everton played Oxford United at the Manor Ground in a Milk Cup (the Football League Cup) fifth-round tie. At half-time, with the game scoreless, Kendall told his players that his job depended on their performance in the next 45 minutes. A few minutes after the break Oxford took the lead and Everton looked dispirited and ragged. With ten minutes left Kevin Brock, Oxford's under-21 England international, tried an ambitious pass back to Steve Hardwick, only to see Adrian Heath intercept to beat the stranded goalkeeper and equalise.

Everton won the replay 4–1 and went on to reach the Milk Cup final where they met Liverpool. Although they lost over two games, Everton had turned the corner. They did win the FA Cup. In 1984–85 they just failed to repeat that feat, losing to Manchester United in extra time in the final, but by that point they were already English champions and Cup Winners Cup holders at the end of the most successful season in their history. Whether they would have kept up their momentum in the European Cup cannot be known, because the Heysel Stadium disaster occurred a few days after and English clubs were banned from Europe – another unforeseen twist in the plot.

So it cannot be regarded as beyond the bounds of possibility that Jock Wallace would have enjoyed a late flourish in his second spell at Ibrox had events shifted in his favour towards the end of

1985–86. The following season Celtic struggled and Davie Hay was ultimately replaced as manager by Billy McNeill.

Without the abandonment of the pay structure at Ibrox, Rangers could not have attracted the top English stars who were exiled from European competition. The best of them would have gone abroad. Souness would probably have returned to England to manage. What might he have done with, say, Spurs, working alongside a receptive chairman in Irvine Scholar to refashion the team around Richard Gough and Graham Roberts?

Had Souness not been lured to Ibrox he would not have been able to tip off his friend, David Murray, that Robert Maxwell was moving to buy Rangers from Lawrence Marlborough in 1987. Had Maxwell gained control at Ibrox, there is more chance that the pension fund would have been plundered than that the club would have lavished money on expensive imports.

Now let us project our imaginary history ahead several years. It is season 1996–97. Caught unawares by the European Union's verdict in the Bosman case and enfeebled by Maxwell's depredations, Rangers are in no position to become big players on the European market although their manager, Alex Totten, begs the trustees on the board for cash. Nor are Celtic, where the old family dynasties have installed seats on the old terracings at both ends of Celtic Park but are struggling to pay for reroofing work.

A combination of poor results and falling attendances – aggravated by a supporters' boycott – sucks Celtic into a crisis. On 5 March 1997, after an emergency meeting of the board the Bank of Scotland is told that the club's debts cannot be met. Celtic are put into the hands of the liquidators. Gerald Weisfeld is urged by his nephew, Michael MacDonald, to invest but the canny Weisfeld realises that to rebuild Celtic Park and pay the salaries needed to lure continental stars to the east end of Glasgow is beyond even his means.

In Bermuda, a childless bachelor called Fergus McCann shakes his head fretfully on hearing the news on the World Service before he returns to the golf course. Back in Glasgow, the Celtic supporters' hopes are raised by reports that a white knight may be at hand. David Murray, the dynamic owner of Ayr United – who have just reached the semi-finals of the Cup Winners Cup after beating Bayern Munich at state of the art Somerset Park with goals from Cadete and Laudrup – is rumoured to be interested.

Neither he nor his manager, Bryan Robson, are available for comment . . .

* * *

'If I had known all of that was going to happen,' says Murdo MacLeod, 'I would probably have been too nervous to score the equaliser against Rangers.' But score it he did. And the rest, as they say in books such as this, is football history.

Murdo MacLeod was sacked as manager of Partick Thistle in May 1997. A month later he was appointed reserve team coach at Celtic.

Packie Bonner

AS a serviceable definition of the back of beyond, Packie Bonner's birthplace will do as well as any. Burtonport lies out on the wild, haunting Atlantic coast of north-west coast Donegal, between Malinmore Head and Bloody Foreland, in the area known as The Rosses. Behind it, a few miles inland, are the Derryveagh Mountains and the Croaghgorm – or as they are called in English, the Blue Stack Mountains. Burtonport looks out on Aran Island, not to be confused with the more famous isles of the same name which are to be found in Galway Bay.

'It is remote, there's no doubt about that,' said Bonner as he conjured images of that wild ocean coastline amongst the soporific surroundings of the Celtic Park boardroom. 'Close to our home there is a beach five miles long which is beautiful to walk on, even in winter when you have gales coming in off the sea. You can walk the length of the beach and not see another soul.'

The towns and villages of this area are well known to several generations of Glaswegians because it was from Donegal more than any other part of Ireland that successive waves of migrants moved to the city from 1848 onwards, driven by lack of work and land, or by evictions and the desire to avoid starvation in the potato famines. Names like Gweedore and Letterkenny still strike nostalgic chords in many Glasgow families.

And for those who think of the Republic as the south of Ireland, it is worth noting that Burtonport is well to the north of Belfast and that most of Donegal is north of counties Fermanagh, Armagh and Down, which is why migrants naturally looked towards Scotland when they uprooted themselves. The sports of the area reflect two contrasting legacies and Packie Bonner, goalkeeper of Celtic and Ireland and the last player to be signed by Jock Stein, was brought up in both traditions.

'Burtonport is a little fishing village but most of the people in the area live outside it and I grew up about a mile from the town,' Bonner says. 'In most of the Republic you might say that Gaelic Athletic Association sports are dominant – hurling and Gaelic football – but not really where I come from. Burtonport was a garrison town, you know, and during the occupation of Ireland a lot of English people lived there so soccer would have been a big thing for them and I think it spread amongst the natives at that time.

'Soccer was very popular around The Rosses, where I lived, but Gaelic was big also – although that would be Gaelic football rather than hurling – and I played both sports right up until I came over here. I have five sisters and a twin brother, Denis. He's the older brother supposedly but there was only a minute or two in it. I used to play football with him and when we were young I was in goals and he was out taking shots at me, so that's how it developed. I suppose you could say that I trained him and he trained me because we both became professional footballers. Denis played for Sligo Rovers, Finn Harps and Galway Rovers.

'I was diving about when I was very young because we didn't have anything like ash parks. It was all grass so if you were in goal you could dive about like a maniac and I think that's where I got my spring. Actually, until I was 12 or 13, whenever I played for a team I was always outfield and never goalkeeper but I was tall and by the time I got to that age I was six feet. I didn't grow much after that but I enjoyed diving about and making the saves so I just stuck with it as a goalkeeper.

'In Gaelic I played outfield – in midfield, actually – so between both sports I got a good range of activities. My primary school played the two sports but mainly football, to be honest. When I was older I went to Donglow Community School but my interest in football was not so much through the school by then as with the local junior team, Keadue Rovers. We started off with the under-16 team and progressed up to the seniors and it was through Keadue Rovers that I developed in soccer.

'I played for my county at both soccer and Gaelic football. The two seemed to go hand in hand in Donegal and what you would find was that most of the guys who were good at soccer could play well at Gaelic also. With Gaelic football being a mixture of hand and foot skills it was helpful to being a soccer goalkeeper and that's one of the reasons I played in midfield. I hated being in goal at Gaelic football because you were tied down too much and you couldn't come out to narrow your angles because then an opponent would just pop the ball over your head and score through the posts above the goal.

'By playing outfield in Gaelic football I could get to catch the ball as well as run around in the middle of the park to get myself fit and strong. I think it was a huge help in developing me so that when I came here I could adjust to the physical side of professional football.

'I was playing football at county level and then at provincial level when Sean Fallon, who was chief scout then and being Irish had very good contacts there, heard about me. A lot of people take credit for getting me recognition but Sean kept an eye on me and he watched me when I got trials for the Irish youth team and again when I got into the youth team. From there he invited me over for trials.

'I came over in 1978, went back to school again in Donglow and at Easter the Irish youth team went to France. Back I went to school after that and then Jock Stein came over with Sean Fallon in May. Of course, I had seen Jock at Celtic Park when I was over on trial but he didn't really have much to do with any of the reserve players at that time. The first team was having a bit of a ropey time during that period and I remember one day when I came in for training I saw him walking up and down on the main park on his own.

'Neil Mochan more or less said to me that if the team had been beaten the night before, don't go near Big Jock. That stood out in my mind and although he introduced himself to me I spoke to him very little. When he came over to Ireland with Sean we met in what is now the Mount Errigal Hotel in Letterkenny after I had got a phone call to say that Celtic wanted to sign me and would I make my way out there to have talks with Jock Stein.

'Jock met Fran Fields, the chairman of Finn Harps, who was a great friend of his and I arrived with my mum, dad and some of the local club officials. To be honest, I didn't think at all about what he was offering me because as far as I was concerned it was a matter of getting myself signed as quickly as possible and that was it. I got £70 a week at that time which wasn't bad considering what a lot of the senior players were earning in those days – not very much, many of them.

'I signed there and then and started my pre-season training in early July. Ironically, by that time Jock was gone, along with Sean Fallon. Billy McNeill had taken over between times.'

Stein's last judgement of an embryonic Celtic player proved to be long-sighted. Bonner was to have a first team career which would begin within eight months and span an immense 17 years. He would take his place alongside Patsy Gallagher and Bertie Peacock as an acquisition from Ireland who repaid the club through long service. With Gallagher, who was born in Milford, 15 miles north of Letterkenny, he shared the distinction of a Donegal birthplace.

With Peacock, who hailed from Coleraine, he had the common experience of finding himself adrift and lonely in Glasgow. In the history of Coleraine FC, the club he managed after leaving Celtic, Peacock has told how he arrived on a morning boat and made his way to the digs which had been arranged for him.

'I stood in the hallway reading the occupants' names, looking for my landlady. A door opened and an elderly woman asked me who I was looking for. When I explained, she told me the woman had been taken ill and rushed into hospital two days earlier.

'If I had had anyone to take me home there and then, I would have gone back,' he recollected of his experience in 1949. Twenty-nine years later Bonner was to undergo the same transition, no less painfully.

Looking back across almost two decades, Bonner remembers clearly the enormous adjustments he was obliged to make to survive his first months in Scotland. 'I found it difficult to deal with it all, very much so. There was a huge, huge difference between Donegal and Glasgow, not just between the places themselves but also between the life I had been used to living and what I could expect over here.

'I had been in Glasgow for trials, of course, and I had also been over at Leicester City a few times for the same reason. I had been away with the Irish youth team as well but I don't think anything prepares you properly for going away from your family for the very first time and it was Christmas before I got back home again.

'To tell you the truth, I was homesick for about the first two years even though I stayed with my uncle and aunt in Glasgow. In fact, I had two sets of uncles and aunts here and I swapped over and went to stay with the other ones later on but I was very, very homesick and I missed my family terribly. The thing about our family was that there were seven of us kids plus my mum and dad and my grandmother, so there were ten of us around the place. And coming from a big family made it worse to be away from them and all my friends.

'If I had been able to see them regularly it would not have been so bad but although my mum and dad came over and back quite a few times there were long gaps sometimes. I look at some of the young kids here now and they come away to us at 16, which is two years younger than I was, and it must be really hard for some of them.

'I was also very close to Denis and having played all our football together and been best of pals, too, that was very, very hard for me. He was still at school and I missed him which heightened all the difficulties for me, but I stuck it out and eventually I settled down as most people do. It was a definite help to get into the first team so quickly because although the demands of playing football every week meant I couldn't get home too much, I also had to concentrate on the job, which took my mind off the problems for at least part of the time.

'Peter Latchford was the first choice goalkeeper when I signed but I got in the following year which, when you think about it now, is a very short space of time to go from being on trial to playing in the first team. Roy Baines was here when I came at first but they sold Roy on around the September after I joined which meant I was second choice goalkeeper. I made my debut on St Patrick's Day 1979 appropriately enough, against Motherwell and we won 2–1. I played the following month and it was Motherwell again because we had a postponed game to get out of the way.

'I didn't play very well – we scored four but I let in three – and then I went out of the team for the rest of that season so that it was really another year before I got back into the team, but to be chosen so quickly after I had signed was quite incredible for me at that time.

'There were big changes at Celtic when Billy McNeill took over. I think Billy looked at everybody in the same light. I've said this before – it seemed to me that he didn't see you as the new boy or the man in possession. As far as he was concerned I was probably the same as Peter Latchford to a certain degree. Billy just wanted to see what abilities everybody had because it was all new to him, so that helped me settle into the first team more easily.

'And then, the defence was full of experienced players. There was Shuggie Edvaldsson, Andy Lynch, Roy Aitken – who was relatively young but who had a lot of experience – Tom McAdam was there, Roddy McDonald, and Danny McGrain, of course. Billy bought in new players and the team clicked very quickly and we went on to win the championship the very first year I was in the side regularly.

'As far as I was concerned I didn't think too much about how I played and what I was supposed to be doing. A lot of times I think that probably let me down but I would say that over the piece it must have been the right thing otherwise I couldn't have kept my place in the team.'

Although it was impossible for them to attend many of Celtic's fixtures, the Bonner family was able to monitor Packie's progress in his adopted home by listening to match commentaries on BBC Radio Scotland and BBC Radio Sport from London, both of which can be heard clearly in most parts of Donegal. 'That was very much the case,' says Bonner. 'In fact, they all missed my debut because there was a strike by Irish post office workers which stopped the telephone services and I didn't really know I was playing until the day before so there was no way I could get in touch with them to get them to come over.

'And they really didn't know until the game was over and they read it in the papers the next day. But after that if they couldn't come over they listened in to the games on the BBC. They still do but, of course, when satellite broadcasting came in it meant that they could watch Celtic games at home. They can analyse your game from a distance a lot better now and maybe look at your faults as well. I think I preferred the radio because you guys don't say too much about the little mistakes.'

There were not too many mistakes for the young goalkeeper once he displaced Peter Latchford and in his first full season – 1980–81 – he did not miss a single game in the championship, League Cup or Scottish Cup. The harmony within the side that season is described by Charlie Nicholas elsewhere in this book but with McGrain, Aitken and McAdam missing only eight games between them there was a dependable platform in defence for a league campaign which ended in a title victory for Celtic.

Their status as champions meant a return to the European Cup but they were drawn against the formidable Juventus and despite a 1–0 home victory in the first leg, courtesy of a Murdo MacLeod goal, Celtic could not sustain their lead in Italy where a 2–0 defeat ended their interest in the competition. McNeill and his players remedied the situation as best they could by retaining the championship and for the second season in succession Bonner was present for every fixture in the three domestic tournaments.

When the draw for the 1982–83 European Cup was made in Switzerland there were few amongst the Celtic support who believed that there was any more chance of a prolonged run than there had been a year previously. Out of Uefa's ballot along with Celtic came Ajax Amsterdam, a team who embodied glamour as well as that much misused term, genius. Johann Cruyff was ageing, but he remained the entrancing master of the Dutch club which won the trophy for three years in a row from 1971.

'The rate at which I found myself playing in big, important matches was incredible. Maybe the reason Jock went was that the team had not been playing to the standards he set and how Celtic performed in Europe was really the measure of that. Billy McNeill had been very disappointed not to have done better against Juventus so although we thought that Ajax would be just as difficult to play against – more so, probably – there was always a belief at Celtic Park that we were a club who counted in Europe and that it was up to us to carry that on.

'When I look back, there were so many huge games that in some ways it is difficult for me to pick a match and say, yes, that was the one. But Europe was always particularly special for Celtic, especially with us having won the European Cup, and I felt you had to make it count as much as possible because this was your reward for all the hard work you had put into winning the championship.

'Celtic supporters dream of another day like Lisbon in 1967 and the players are exactly the same. Every time we played in Europe I thought of that achievement and wondered how it would feel if we could do that, too. But this particular draw against Ajax was even more special than most because they had won the cup and we had won it and both clubs knew the feeling of being the best, the very best in Europe.

'The two games against them have always been important to me, partly for what we achieved against a team of Ajax's class. Personally, the second leg in Holland remains fresh in my memory because it was responsible for setting my career off in another direction which didn't seem very likely at the time. When the draw was made our first reaction was to say that they never seemed to give us an easy passage to the quarter-finals of the European Cup.

'It certainly looked as if we might be going out in the first round again after the first leg here. To be honest, they were wonderful, they truly were wonderful. I thought maybe at the start of the game they might be a bit unsettled because their regular goalkeeper, Piet Schrijvers, who played for Holland, injured himself in the warm-up and they had to bring in another lad, Hans Galje.

'That was something we thought we could maybe capitalise on and we wanted to test the goalie as early as possible but it didn't quite work out the way we had planned.'

Certainly, Celtic went instantly upfield from the start and in the first minute, with the crowd of 57,000 in exceptional voice behind them, McNeill's men twice lanced through an Ajax defence which looked ponderously square. Both attacks created good goalscoring chances. Both fell to Frank McGarvey and each time he shot straight at Galje. The keeper had been tested but instead of being unnerved he was now buoyed with confidence.

Having survived those first two frights Ajax retorted in the same fashion, but more spectacularly. In the fourth minute, the mercurial Danish winger, Jesper Olsen, broke down the left beating McGrain and Moyes before squeezing his shot between Bonner and his right-hand post. Celtic had not merely conceded the feared away goal to Ajax, they were also chasing the game against players of pace and vision who were adept at landing the damaging counter-punch. As Celtic began to haul themselves back into the game Galje made an outstanding save from a typically venomous Davie Provan free kick.

Celtic supporters who had read their newspapers carefully on the morning of the game – the death of Princess Grace in a car crash in Monaco had dominated the front page headlines – knew that Cruyff had been out of action for six weeks because of an ankle injury but that the 35-year-old Dutch international was effectively in charge of the team rather than the coach, Aad de Mos. Cruyff had pronounced himself fit to play at Celtic Park but whether he overestimated his own powers of recovery or his timing was slipping slightly with age, he effectively cancelled Ajax's advantage before quarter of an hour had been played.

Celtic won a corner kick on the left which Provan played short to Tommy Burns, who surged into the box only to be tripped by

Cruyff for a clear penalty kick. Charlie Nicholas beat Galje easily and bedlam broke out with renewed vigour around the packed terracings.

'I thought when Charlie scored from the penalty kick that now we had a chance to settle into the game the way we wanted to do at the start but we had hardly equalised when they were back in the lead,' Bonner remembers.

'I think we were maybe a bit slack in covering but Cruyff got the ball from Olsen and he knocked it on to Lerby. I had to come out to try to block him but he chipped the ball over me into the net. So we had to start to chase them all over again but we did it and made it 2–2 before the half hour, as I remember.'

To be precise, it was in 27 minutes that Davie Moyes headed beyond the Ajax defenders into space for McGarvey to go clear on goal. It was his third look at the target with only Galje to stop him and this time McGarvey drove his shot low under the goalkeeper and Celtic were level again.

'You would have thought it might have calmed down a wee bit after that but actually it never let up. They were fast and very good on the ball. There weren't many people who could give Danny McGrain a hard time but Olsen did that night, even though he got a couple of hard knocks doing it. He would show the ball to Danny and go past him to set up a chance. They didn't ease up until late in the game when I suppose they thought that a draw would do them, especially with the two away goals. They had made a couple of chances which could easily have won them the game because Schoenaker hit our bar with a header and I made a good save from Lerby in the second half.'

Celtic were not exactly bereft of opportunities themselves and Galje had to make a fine stop to to prevent Nicholas from scoring with a shot on the run. Tommy Burns insisted afterwards that he should have had another penalty kick when Olsen brought him down late in the proceedings, but there was no further scoring and the game ended in a 2–2 draw which favoured Ajax.

'I wasn't surprised that the newspapers and probably most of our fans thought that we had lost our chance because they had looked so skilful that you would have to have fancied them at home, especially since we had gone out to Juventus the year before after we had won at Celtic Park, an advantage we didn't have in this case.

'The players were never despondent about it, though. We knew that a draw wouldn't be any use to us unless it was a high-scoring draw, which was very unlikely, so we were going to have to go there and win. But most of us felt that we would score over there and if that happened we would be in with a good chance again.

'So over we went and the night before the game we trained in the ground where the game was going to be played, which was the Olympic Stadium. I always liked to train on the pitch we would be playing on. When you saw the stadium empty it was a good way to get the adrenalin going, not that we needed to do that in this case.

'While we were getting the feel of the place I noticed that the goal areas were slightly raised above the rest of the pitch and I pointed this out to Charlie Nicholas. There was a little slope running away from the goalmouth and I said to Charlie that maybe if he could get their goalkeeper coming off his line he could use this to knock the ball over him. I don't know whether or not he listened to me but it turned out to be a good tip.'

Earlier on that day before the game Billy McNeill had been asked what strategy Celtic would employ. He replied: 'Our main job is to take their creative players out of the game. Then we have to hope that our front men can produce the kind of magic that Olsen did at Celtic Park. Charlie Nicholas can do it. He is capable of snatching a goal in any company. It would be perfect if we could start the game the way Ajax started against us.'

What is the famous dictum about a manager having no control over what happens once his players step over that white line? On this occasion McNeill offered such an exact preview of what was to happen that he appears to have experienced a vision of the game.

Bonner takes up the story again: 'Our hotel wasn't very far from the Olympic Stadium and Billy usually gave us the team talk in the hotel because you never knew what distractions there might be when you got to the ground. (*Author's note: See also Davie Provan's account of a fraught European Cup night in Dundalk elsewhere in this book.*)

'When we got to the ground I used to concentrate on my stretching exercises and so on. It was Danny McGrain who showed me how important it was to have a routine you could get into before the match so that you were mentally prepared to go out there and play whatever the circumstances might be.

'When the game started we were in amongst them right away and we got a couple of corner kicks pretty quickly but they were as lively as they had been in the first leg and Olsen made one of his good runs to give Schoenaker a chance. He hit a good shot and I had to go full length to reach it, which was good for me because it gave me an early feel of the ball and I think that it is always important for a goalkeeper, especially in an important match.

'We were doing very well but for a lot of the time it was very much a case of our backs to the wall. Then after half an hour or so, Charlie Nicholas scored. If you remember what I had told him about the goal areas, well, lo and behold . . .'

To quote Ken Gallacher's description of the move in the *Daily Record* : 'It began with a glorious pass across the park from Paul McStay. The ball found Graeme Sinclair who abandoned his role of shadowing Johann Cruyff to burst forward down the left side. He sent the ball to Nicholas who picked it up and weaved past two tackles. He passed to Frank McGarvey, took a return ball and then coolly and clinically chipped it over the head of Piet Schrijvers in the Ajax goal.

'It was an impressive first half from Celtic. In contrast, when the Dutchmen did go forward they found Bonner looking confident. He saved from Molby and Olsen and when Cruyff sent Boeve clear the big keeper pulled the ball out of the air though he had been fouled by Schoenaker.'

Bonner's memory of his interventions – and Nicholas's contribution – is clear after almost a decade and a half: 'I'm not likely to forget Charlie's goal because he scored by putting it over their keeper's head as he came off his line. I can't remember if Charlie ever thanked me for the advice but I can tell you this, we were all so busy thanking him for what he had done afterwards he could hardly have got a word in edgeways.

'I had a lot of good saves that night and I remember one in particular just after half-time. They were desperate to get a goal back and they came at us right away. A free kick was given against Paul McStay just outside our penalty area in a dangerous position. They had a few players who could be dangerous in these situations but in this case Cruyff decided he was going to take it.

'He swerved it around our wall and I saw it coming late but I was able to get down away to my left and touch it on to the post and luckily it rebounded the right way for us. That was the closest they got for a while but they had us pinned back and Olsen was giving Danny another difficult evening.

'He was involved in the move which led to their equaliser. They were playing short passes around our box, then they got into our area and Vandenburg tried a shot which squeezed through a bunch of players and curled in off the back post. It was a fluke goal but it put them back in front on the away goals rule.

'It got very tense after that because another goal either way was going to settle the match. Cruyff got injured in the middle of the pitch with a couple of minutes to go and, of course, he made the most of it. Eventually, they helped him very slowly off to the side and they must have thought that they had wasted just about enough time to take them up to the final whistle.

'There was nothing else for us to do but have a go at them and it was one of those moments where you thought, right, this has got to be our last chance, please let it go in because if it does they'll never have time to come back from that. George McCluskey had come on as a substitute and I think some of the papers gave him credit for making the winning goal and scoring it but my memory of it was that Danny McGrain tried a shot and George deflected it in.

'He was good at that – he did it in the 1980 Scottish Cup final when we beat Rangers. Then the referee blew for time and our lot went crazy. There were about 2,000 Celtic supporters in the stadium and they were all you could hear apart from a few Dutch fans booing. Mostly they were throwing cushions or standing silent.

'I can still see some of our players sitting on the grass as if they couldn't believe what they had done. They were just drained of all their energy. Billy McNeill and the others who had been on the bench ran on to the pitch and they were hugging everybody. Johann Cruyff was limping up the side trying not to look at anyone.

'Then we went off back to our hotel for a bit of a celebration. Billy was on a huge high because we had beaten Ajax when most people had written us off and I think we all felt we had shown we had learned from the games against Juventus the year before. Also, in both games Ajax had played really well, just as we had expected, but we came from behind again and again to beat them. It was about as marvellous a fighting performance as you could have wanted from any team, the kind of football that had made Celtic famous in Europe under Jock Stein and now we had done it as well.

'But the real bonus for me came afterwards. Eoin Hand was the manager of Ireland then but he had never seen me play for Celtic. To be honest, I had got a bit peeved about this. Whether it was

because he didn't really rate me or whether he thought Scottish
football wasn't worth his while, I don't know but anyway he never
showed up at Celtic Park, although he had given me a few games
for Ireland.

'However, he was also the manager of Limerick and they had a
game in Holland at the same time but not on the same night as us.
So he came along on spec really, but what he saw put me in his
thoughts properly and I was back in the Irish team the next year.
I got into the Celtic first team for the first time on St Patrick's Day
and I played my first game for Ireland on my 21st birthday, 24
May 1981 and I got another cap against Algeria in Algiers in April
the following year, but they were both friendlies and Eoin
preferred Seamus McDonagh for most games.'

Now at this point we must leave Bonner's account because there
is a gap which can be filled in by Charlie Stewart, the veteran Irish
football writer who graced the pages of the *Irish Press* until it
folded in 1994. Stewart, a Scottish expatriate (though his brogue
now owes more to Dublin than to his native Aberdeenshire), had
been insistent that Hand should give Bonner a chance in a
competitive game.

'I was always on at Eoin Hand to go and look at Packie Bonner
but he had no regard for Scottish football. He just wouldn't go and
watch Packie over there and I don't think he ever saw Celtic play
at home in his life,' says Stewart. 'But that was an attitude which
was hard to justify when Packie was part of a Celtic team which
won the Scottish championship in successive seasons while
Ireland were using a goalkeeper who was playing for Notts County
reserves and even their third team.

'He did give him a couple of caps in games which didn't matter
much but that was done to placate a lot of people. He obviously
wasn't convinced that this young lad from Donegal had what it
took or was likely to have it. There was one honey of a game when
Trinidad and Tobago beat Ireland 2–1 – Liam Brady got the goal
and he had plenty to say about the way the Irish set-up was being
run on that occasion – and Gerry Payton was in goal. That was
about four months before Celtic played Ajax in Amsterdam.

'Anyway, when Celtic went to Holland, Eoin didn't have an
excuse not to go along and watch because Limerick had a second
leg game against AZ Alkmaar the next day.

'At the end of the game in Amsterdam, when Celtic had beaten
Ajax, he was totally taken aback. I said, "I've been telling you

about Packie for a couple of years – now will you believe me?" I was very proud of my goalkeeper. That's how I thought of him – as my goalkeeper.

'I remember Packie saying to me afterwards, "Well, I hope that impressed him." And it did, it did, because Eoin went back to the Celtic hotel to speak to him after the game. Seamus McDonagh kept his place in the side for a wee while but Packie started to appear for Ireland more regularly after that, although Gerry Payton of Fulham got a couple of caps as well.

'Now, I'll tell you something about Packie. Because I know him pretty well I must have had a hundred offers to write a book with him, but he won't do it and the reason is that if you do a book like that and be honest with your readers, you're going to have to criticise some of the people you've come across in your career. And Packie refuses to do that. He's that kind of person.

'But I can say that Eoin Hand was wrong to have kept him out of the Irish team as much as he did. It was a misjudgement. When Jack Charlton took over in 1986 he gave Gerry Payton a game and then in his second match in charge he put Packie in goal and he stayed there for ten years.'

True to Charlie Stewart's prediction, Bonner declines to indict Hand with negligence of his potential. 'I've had a very good career and most things have worked out well for me so I'm not inclined to start criticising from a distance.

'I was only a young goalkeeper at the time. Eoin Hand was the manager of Ireland and entitled to his opinion. He picked the team and he took the responsibility for the results, not me. What I would say was that he did come back to the hotel and speak to me after the Ajax game and my performance that night definitely put me higher in his thoughts.

'It didn't mean I was into the Irish team right away. Seamus more or less kept his place but he was eight years older than me and most managers like to be able to bank on experience when they're playing European Championship or World Cup qualifiers.

'The thing about the game against Ajax for me was that it showed that I could play well at that level and as far as Celtic were concerned it proved that we were still capable of being a force in European football. If I have one disappointment in my career as a Celtic player it's that I won't be playing when the ground is rebuilt. Roy Aitken and I were talking about this recently. The atmosphere here was always fantastic on European nights and we probably didn't think it could ever be surpassed, but with the new Celtic Park it will be. That's a certainty.

'There's no question about it. And this club is just too big now not to be a force in Europe again. After all, look at Ajax, the team we beat on their own ground that night. They came back to be the best club side in the world. So it can be done. We've never had more season ticket holders, we've never had a stadium this good, we've never had so much money coming into the club.

'Tommy Burns has even been over to Holland a few times to study Ajax's methods. We were the first British team to win the European Cup and the Dutch learned from us. Why shouldn't Celtic return the favour?'

And as for Bonner and Ireland . . . he now coaches the Irish goalkeepers. Comments about traditions and safe hands are superfluous.

Billy McNeill

CELTIC 4 RANGERS 2

21 May 1979

If you can make one heap of all your winnings
And risk it on one turn of pitch and toss ...
Rudyard Kipling

ON a Monday evening in May 1979 the heap of Celtic's winnings permitted them to stand above every other team in the premier division. With 35 games played only one side – Rangers – could possibly dislodge them and snatch the title away from the east end of Glasgow. Under John Greig, in his first season as manager, Rangers were bidding for a second successive treble but if Celtic were to lose the league they would finish with nothing in the trophy cabinet.

It had been a peculiar championship campaign, distorted by the severe winter which had badly affected the Old Firm's schedules so that Rangers played only three league fixtures between 23 December and 14 March while Celtic managed none at all between Christmas and 3 March. In fact, when Celtic restarted their programme they were close to the foot of the table, although the situation was misleading because of the number of postponed games which had built up.

By 21 May Celtic had only match left to play – against Rangers at Parkhead. The success or failure of Celtic's season now depended on the outcome of these final 90 minutes and there was no scope for error because although Rangers were three points behind they had two games in hand. In other words, a win for Rangers would almost guarantee that they would retain the title and a draw would still make them favourites for another championship.

Some observers described this match as the equivalent of a cup final but a final by definition is the culmination of a knockout tournament which rarely requires either of the contenders to play more than half a dozen ties. A championship, on the other hand, is a true test of adaptability, beginning on the manicured pitches of late summer and progressing through the strength-sapping winter muds and flint hard tops on to the rutted surfaces of spring.

For the fans, the prospect of a league title is the ultimate reward for freezing afternoons and bitter nights spent along the familiar football trade routes from Aberdeen to Ayrshire. The fulfilment of nine long months of concentrated work and devotion on and off the field was at stake for both sides.

Like Greig, Billy McNeill was in his first season as an Old Firm manager, but unlike the former Rangers captain he had gained managerial experience away from the club he had served so impressively as player and skipper and he had earned favourable notices for his work at Clyde and Aberdeen.

'I had been through something like this the previous season with Aberdeen,' McNeill recollected, as we talked in his pub on the south side of Glasgow, close to Hampden Park. It is, as you would expect, something of a Celtic shrine, the walls adorned with team pictures and match programmes. In such a setting, memories are easily evoked.

'When I was manager of Aberdeen we finished as runners-up to Rangers and what worried me was that we had enjoyed a long spell of victories in the league and we never lost a game in the second half of the season until Rangers beat us in the Cup final, yet we ended up second in the table two points behind them. So when it happened again with Celtic I had become used to it but I had also found that when you're chasing, the pressure is not as great. All you can do is go out and play your best and hope for the other team to make the mistake.

'At Celtic, just the same as at Aberdeen, we had a long, successful run towards the end of the season but I always remember that earlier we had been due to play Rangers at Ibrox. This was at the time when Ibrox was being reconstructed and they elected to play the game at Hampden Park. On the Wednesday night before the Old Firm game they had a European Cup-tie against Cologne and they got some great publicity from the fact that they had used lots of local schoolboys to clear the pitch of snow.

'Now when it came to the game at Hampden there was a bit of snow on the pitch but the weather forecast was good and it was clearing up rapidly. Rangers nevertheless had the game called off on the basis of public safety. Fair enough, I'm not criticising them for that but it meant that they started to get involved in a backlog of postponed games and what created the opportunity for us was that our good run put pressure on them. We whittled away their lead and although they had games in hand, suddenly it all came to a climax with us going in to our last game at home knowing we needed a victory, whereas they knew that they could get by with a draw.

'I honestly felt that whatever pressure was on both sides, they would feel it more than we did. We had a terrific build-up. When you're going well and you're on a good run everything is easy, nothing goes wrong in training and the atmosphere around the place is good. Every manager of a successful side talks about the team spirit but I felt ours was exceptional at the time.

'We were a young side when you consider it. I mean, if you take Danny McGrain and Andy Lynch out of that side we had a fair amount of youngsters, people like Davie Provan and Murdo MacLeod, who were in their first season at the club but who had already shown us that they were superb players. I just felt that suddenly we had a chance.

'So we were going into a match against our greatest rivals with so much at stake and I had often heard Jock Stein say that a Rangers game wasn't any more important than playing against any other side. Well, big Jock may have said that but he certainly didn't mean it because the importance of that game was never lost on us. You don't have to build players up before any Old Firm derby but this one was in a class of its own.

'We knew what it was worth and Rangers knew it, too. We had the extra element of young men who realised that if they could give us something special on this evening then they would do a lot for their future in the game. I've mentioned Provan and MacLeod but I mustn't forget George McCluskey, too. Mind you, no matter how eager the younger lads might be we needed experience for this one and, again, we had that in abundance. I've been speaking about McGrain and Lynch in defence but there was also big Johannes Edvaldsson, who had served us very well and who knew exactly what it was all about.

'Either way, the feeling I had was that we had an awful lot of players with a great appetite to play for Celtic. I think the run of success that Rangers have enjoyed in recent years is down to the fact that they have a solid core of players who feel for the club and know what it means to their supporters. We certainly had that in abundance that night.

'But in a highly charged situation like that you mustn't let the atmosphere take control of your emotions and when I spoke to them in the dressing-room before they went out I warned them of that. Yet no matter how much you tell players, once they go on to the pitch it can be very hard for them not to give in to it at some point or other and we lost Johnny Doyle when he got himself sent off for aiming a kick at Alex MacDonald.

'To be fair to Johnny, he had been subjected to some fairly harsh treatment but as so often happens, as soon as you retaliate – bingo! You go off. Now I couldn't really criticise his reaction in one way, but I had warned them all and he hadn't got the message. Plus the fact, we were 1–0 down to a goal scored by Alex MacDonald in the first half and here we were reduced to ten men not long after half-time, so I said to Johnny as he wandered over to make his way up the tunnel, I said to him, "Doylie, I hope to hell we win because if we don't you're in trouble."

'You see, at half-time I had told them to forget the fact we were losing, that it was relatively unimportant that we were a goal down because if you fall behind in an Old Firm game you can only go one way. I felt it suited us and the way we liked to play that Rangers might try to defend their lead. So I wasn't too troubled until Johnny went off. Any sympathy I had for him disappeared because professionally it's just something you shouldn't get involved in.

'So he wandered off looking fairly worried but now I had to ask myself how I could change things on the pitch to make up for what had happened. I had Mick Conroy playing, another youngster and one of the nicest guys the world has ever known but I felt I needed mobility. There was George McCluskey who was terrific at leading the line – you could put the ball to his feet and he would control it – but what we needed was people who would run their backsides off and Johnny Doyle going off had lost us a lot of pace and sharpness.

'Basically, what I did was to leave George McCluskey up by himself, take Mick Conroy off and replace him with Bobby Lennox, who went over to one side with Davie Provan on the other, and I said right, just push up from that midfield area – and it worked a treat for us. How many times have we said that there is a real impact on a team playing with ten men against eleven? I think part of it is that when defenders aren't playing against a full quota of attackers, they find it difficult.

'It might be one of the reasons that European teams play with one centre forward and leave other people to get up and support him. At any rate, as I say, the arrangement worked very well for us that night because not only were Davie Provan and Bobby Lennox up there supporting him, but so too was Roy Aitken. Roy in that match was a gargantuan figure and he must have covered every single inch of the ground. Midway through the half up he goes, gets a header in and we're at 1–1.

'So now the game is going our way and the crowd are wild but we also know that a draw is no use to us and time is ebbing away. That's when both dugouts start looking at the time a great deal and with 15 minutes left we scored again. George McCluskey was due some reward for the work he had put in to keep the Rangers defenders occupied and I was very glad for him that he was the one to put us ahead.

'Of course, as soon as you take the lead you're apt to worry that you'll lose it again, which would give the other team an even greater boost than you have just had. I remember Frank Connor sitting in our dugout saying to me after George's goal, "Billy, that's it – the big fella up the stairs is on our side tonight."

'And what happened? Rangers go up the park, get a corner kick and Bobby Russell scores to bring them level again. I turned to Frank and said, "Well, the big fella's making an awful hard job of it, is he not?"

'The game went crazy after that, just racing from end to end and back again. Anybody who had come in without knowing what was going on would have been forgiven for not noticing that we were a man short because it didn't seem to be important. For all you could tell, it was having no effect on us at all unless it was making us play even better than some of the lads ever imagined they could. And all the time the crowd is going bananas and the noise is unbelievable.

'What you might not have expected was that the quality of the football was so high on both sides. The standard of the game was absolutely magnificent. Of course, time was running away fast and it was still 2–2 with only seven minutes left. In any football game but especially in an Old Firm game seven minutes can be an eternity. The world can explode in seven minutes and certainly the world around Parkhead exploded that night.

'You know, the thing which struck me so forcibly as we moved into the last few minutes was that by going 2–1 ahead we had got a helluva lift but equally the impact of them scoring an equaliser could have been too much of a drop for us. But our team could have taken anything and come back that night. I remember they had an attack down their right-hand side, our left, and Bobby Russell had got himself free and was boring into the box.

'And I saw this figure flying across the pitch and slamming into the tackle. I couldn't believe my eyes – it was Davie Provan. Now how the hell he got there, I don't know. I asked him and he couldn't tell me. I couldn't tell you. Nobody has ever been able to tell me, because he was actually playing on the right side of the pitch for us and he came steaming right across the park and put in this perfect saving tackle.

'That was one example of the way we were playing. I think all of our players took on an added dimension in that game. So seven minutes left and we score again, or rather Rangers score for us. It was one of those difficult things if you've been a player yourself, especially playing in the same position as the man who scores an own goal because you know just what it must feel like.

'It was Colin Jackson who put it past his own goalkeeper. It came from a cross from George McCluskey and Peter McCloy came out to push it away but it came off Colin Jackson and into his own net. However much I was elated by the goal I was saying to myself, oh, what a sad thing for that big fella. And funnily enough, he said to Bobby Lennox on the pitch, "I hope to God you score another goal or else we score another one because I'd hate to be remembered as the man who lost the league for Rangers."

'I could understand that. He got his wish, mind you, although not with the choice he would have made because almost on time Murdo MacLeod strode forward and Murdo – well, what a superb striker of the ball he was, and what a contribution he made that evening from midfield – was making ground and myself, John Clark, Neil Mochan, Bob Rooney were all shouting, "Shoot! Shoot!"

'We weren't thinking that he would score necessarily. It was more that the old Celtic Park had the big wide open ends so if he missed the target – and to be honest with you, we weren't that sure that Murdo would hit the target – the ball would have gone away up into the terracing somewhere and the supporters would have made sure it didn't come back too quickly and we would have lost another few seconds. The ball boys hopefully wouldn't have been hurrying too much either.

'But we needn't have worried because Murdo slammed it straight into the net. It was a fabulous drive and he remembers it to this day, let me tell you. Once that went past Peter McCloy we knew it was all over and from then on it was championship time and we could celebrate all we wanted. The ball probably gathered another 20 miles an hour on the way because the fans were roaring it into the net.

'They made a helluva contribution the fans. We used to think the stadium had a lot to do with it, the big terracings, the sweep of the ground but I think you have to say it's really down to the supporters because the atmosphere in the new stadium is absolutely dynamic. The Celtic fans are awful good at certain things. They sense when they're needed, they know when to respond and all they're looking for in return is a response from the players on the pitch.

'That night the players and the supporters gave each other everything they could have asked for. I've played in many, many games with dramatic finishes and famous results but I doubt very much if I've ever experienced anything as exhilarating or as exciting as that game. It was utterly exhausting. It didn't stop with the final whistle, either, because even after we had done our lap of honour and eventually got back into the dressing-room the door kept bursting open and in would come one former Celtic player after another.

'And it was a case of "Come on, come on – everybody in!" Because it was one of those occasions which belonged to everybody who ever had played for the club or supported it as well as those who were on the field or the terracings that evening. We had been a goal down and a man down to a Rangers side which was going for the treble and we had ended up scoring four against them.

'As you know, Greigy and I have always been great friends and still are. That night I felt sympathy for him because having had a relationship with him for so long I could understand his emotions. He took it brilliantly although, obviously, inside he must have been sick to the soles of his feet. But I think it was one of those days when our name was pure and simply written on the championship and I'm sure Greigy knew it, too.

'He came over and shook my hand at full-time and congratulated me. I phoned John afterwards to say, look, I fully appreciate how you feel but more importantly you made yourself a right big man by accepting it in the way you did. And I have to be honest and say there were maybe not so many people waiting to join that queue.

'There's a fairytale aspect of Celtic which shows itself every now and again and that was another of our wee tales which will be remembered as long as anyone is alive who was there to see it. I hadn't thought at all about what would happen if we had lost because when I came from Aberdeen the Celtic team I inherited was at its lowest position in the league for many years, so basically anything we could do near the top of the table would be an improvement.

'We had already had a rather eventful League Cup semi-final against Rangers that season when they had Alex Miller sent off and we had Tommy Burns dismissed. We felt the decision about Tommy was unfair and wrong and unjustified and obviously all these things were in the background, although I tend to think that events even themselves out over the course of a season and in the end, we couldn't have been more satisfied with what we got.'

In the companion book to this volume – *True and Blue,* an account of unforgettable Rangers games, it was put to John Greig that the two Old Firm meetings of the 1970s which could reasonably be described as epic contests were the victory remembered by Billy McNeill in this chapter and Greig's choice, the 1973 Scottish Cup final which Rangers won 3–2. Greig replied that the only epic Old Firm derbies were those you won.

'That's for sure,' says McNeill. 'You can recount the ones you win, usually in great detail, but the ones you lose, you kick them into touch somewhere away at the back of your mind. John's dead right and that's what I was getting at earlier when I said that anybody who believes that an Old Firm game is just another match with three points at stake is kidding themself. It is by a long way the most important domestic fixture of the season even if we play each other half a dozen times in the championship and both the cups, say, and it's remarkable how often they turn out to be so important that they're set apart even from other Old Firm games.

'And the really big games are surrounded by an atmosphere which can be felt even when there is nobody in the ground. Obviously, I would be at the ground hours before the fans would turn up but even then the stadium would tell you that there was going to be a big, big event that day. The stadium knows and is ready for it.

'The stadium talks. It does talk and it sings even when it's empty. And it tells you . . . you better get ready because there's going to be a helluva lot of things happening here today. I've been so fortunate when I look back on my career because although I've had downs – and some of them have been terrible downs – they only made the ups so much better. But even our European Cup win in 1967 I don't believe was emotionally as demanding or exhausting as that Old Firm game.

'I think it was because we hadn't been expected to do well while Rangers had been sailing through the season. Maybe some people thought it would be a cursory exercise, that Rangers would turn up at Celtic Park, get at least a draw and go on to win the league. But that did not happen and the impact on our supporters for such a long time afterwards was quite staggering.'

The victory and the manner of its accomplishment also served to convince Celtic supporters that the club had secured a charismatic successor to Jock Stein. This was the man who was – and remains – the British footballer who accumulated more medals than any other. The first British player to lift the European Cup. Nine championship triumphs, seven Scottish Cup medals and six in the Scottish League Cup were assembled from 24 major cup final appearances in over 800 games for the club.

His last game for Celtic was the Scottish Cup final of 1975, in which Celtic beat Airdrie 3–1. On 1 April 1977, he was appointed manager of Clyde. Ten weeks later he succeeded Ally McLeod as Aberdeen manager. Within 11 months he was back at Celtic, inheritor of a legend he had helped to create, keenly aware that in every detail of his stewardship he would be compared to the Big Man who had been the most succesful manager in Scottish football.

'I was young. I was only 38 years of age. I had enjoyed a good year at Aberdeen and a relatively successful one, finishing second in the league and losing in the Cup final. Pittodrie had been a hard breeding ground for me and a hard year of experience for me in some ways but it was wonderful, too.

'In retrospect – and we're all helluva clever people when we look back – it wasn't the right time to go to Celtic Park for me. I'm talking purely personally now, but I should have stayed at

Aberdeen. I was very happy there, I had a terrific board there and it would have been an ideal proving ground for me. Careerwise, it was wrong for me to move.

'But having said that, it's easy to look back, to be sensible and use the head, but I thought emotionally and when I went to Celtic Park I couldn't believe what had happened. The Celtic Park I had left in 1975 was a place crammed with real quality players but when I came back the good players had gone. Dalglish was away, McGrain and Stanton were injured and the quality men seemed to have disappeared.

'I remember a newspaper report which said I had taken a ruthless approach, something I never thought of until I read that. But it was ruthless because I decided that I had to get new blood in and I was lucky there were players like Provan and MacLeod available. Funnily enough, when I looked at Murdo he was at Dumbarton and they had Graeme Sharp up front. I fancied him as well but I thought, no, there's no way Dumbarton could have two quality youngsters in their side, but I was wrong as he proved when he went down to Everton where he was such a success. I've often thought what might have happened if I had taken both of them.

'Anyway, I then had a look at the other players on the staff and those I didn't think were good enough I just cleared out. I had one stroke of luck. Tom McAdam had come in as a centre forward, a nice player and smashing lad, but not good enough for Celtic as a centre forward. I told Tom I didn't think he would make it as a forward but I had a wee idea in my head and I asked him if he would mind playing in the reserves as a centre half – and he was a natural.

'I know a lot of people criticised him but I always felt he was a better player than was appreciated and he was a very important member of my side in those early years. The thing is, I had never thought of taking over Celtic from big Jock because he had brought me to Celtic Park and he was instrumental to my development as a player. However, it was Jock who came to me and said that the job at Celtic Park was going to come up and that the directors wanted me to come back.

'And I wish he had never said it because I couldn't have refused him. Realistically, you should map out your career and try and get the proper experience but one of the problems with that kind of offer was that I couldn't have known if the job was going to come up again. Politically, though, it was not a good time to be at the club and apart from that I had stopped too early because I know I could have played on. Yet you hate being called a veteran and the boys I had played with had pretty well all gone, so maybe it was the frustration of that coming through, but all I seemed to do for those first five years was to argue with the then chairman, Desmond White.

'I felt – in fact, I know – that he wasn't progressive enough. I said to him one day, "Mr White, you and I should be on the same side but all we seem to do is spend our time fighting. Whenever I want something to improve this side I have to fight a case and it becomes stormy and I don't honestly think that's the answer." When I left to go to Manchester City it was put down to an argument over money but it was nothing to do with that at all. It was an argument about ambition and progress.

'Maybe if I had worked with Dick Donald and Chris Anderson at Aberdeen for a longer period it would have sharpened my abilities as a manager. I look at Alex Ferguson who came after me and he was young, ambitious and aggressive. He went to Aberdeen at the right time because as far as I am concerned they had the two best directors in Scotland. They taught him a lot and on that basis I denied myself their experience.

'Undoubtedly, it is far better to be manager of Celtic now than it was then. The thing which used to annoy me was that I could see all sorts of clubs trying to improve their lot. Never mind Rangers – they were ahead of everybody in this country by far – it was clubs like Ipswich and Norwich who were building new grounds who were starting to leave us behind. I went down to Norwich and got a copy of plans for their new stand and brought it back up here to try to force it on to Desmond White.

'They refused to have undersoil heating. I mean, they didn't even have central heating in the place. It used to drive me daft because I could see that the way ahead was development because with the support and the potential income Celtic could derive from that support, there was only one way to go. Thank God now that this little man, Fergus McCann, has come along because without him . . . what? And Brian Dempsey, too, because Brian gets a lot of credit for what he did to change Celtic, particularly in the early stages.

'It must be very exciting for Tommy Burns because he can now look at quality players. One of the biggest frustrations for me was that I always had to buy at the bargain basement. I bought Paul Elliot and Frank McAvennie and they were very good buys for this club but with players it's like everything else, there are very few bargains available. Tommy doesn't have to scrabble at the bottom of the market and the most heartening thing about Celtic is that although there obviously isn't a bottomless well of money, there is an obvious direction and a solid base to the club.'

The story of McNeill's abrupt departure in July 1983 is familiar to Celtic supporters as are the circumstances of his return in May 1987, when he succeeded Davie Hay and became the only man to manage the club twice. His recall can now be seen as a bid by the directors to summon up the past in an attempt to ward off the future – in the shape of resurgent Rangers under Graeme Souness. Rangers' grip of the championship over the next decade was broken only once, when McNeill supervised a league and cup double in the emotionally supercharged centenary year of 1988, but although Celtic supporters will be perpetually grateful to him for that feat, it was beyond any Parkhead manager to take on the Ibrox juggernaut without the growing resources which were available to Souness.

Celtic were rooted in a dynastic system founded in the 19th century. Rangers were exploiting the corporate resources of the 20th century to prepare for the 21st. Two seasons without a trophy between 1989 and 1991 brought McNeill's second tenure to an inevitable close. Like Hay before him, he refused to accommodate an increasingly beleaguered board by resigning.

'I'm not any different from anybody else. The last thing you enjoy is getting the sack, but you appreciate it if it's done in the proper manner. I was subjected to a chief executive coming in – I can't remember his name – and all that seemed to happen at Celtic Park from that day on was subterfuge and rumours. Now whether those directors and that chief executive were naive, I will leave others to decide, but I had contacts in the press who told me what was going on but what was most offensive about that board was that nobody was prepared to sit down and say, "Look, Billy, this is happening and that is happening, which we don't want."

'They could have got me to say, "Aye, you're dead right. I'm away." Had the situation been treated more sensibly and sympathetically I would have been the first to say, "All right, that's your decision. I'm offski." But the first year I came back not only were two top-class strikers disappearing in Mo Johnston and

Brian McClair but I also lost out on Murdo MacLeod and it was all down to a little manoeuvring on financial terms which I couldn't achieve.

'All of a sudden things went brilliantly for us and we were a good side but we had a lot of players who needed improved upon. I went in at the end of that season when we won the league and cup with incredible gates and asked for money to buy four or five players. They offered me £1 million to pay for them. Now even allowing for cheaper deals in those days, £1 million was a pittance. It might not have been enough to pay for signing-on fees for good quality players.

'Rangers then kept pushing the market just that bit further every time. They bought the best of the English players at that time, which was an astonishing turnaround, but they did it because they knew that was the way ahead and that their ground was going to be top drawer and that they had the financial structure to pay for it all in front of us. Yet the Celtic directors still thought we should be shopping at Paddy's Market.'

Celtic were sent into a tailspin of decline which brought the club to within minutes of unthinkable bankruptcy by two events within the space of three months. One was the Hillsborough Disaster in April 1989 and the other was Mo Johnston's decision to join Rangers six weeks after he had signed for Celtic.

'Maurice Johnston was our player. We had it confirmed by Fifa after he signed a letter of agreement. Now whatever people think, a letter of agreement is a contract. Celtic had paid Nantes a deposit of £400,000 in a £1.2 million deal and all they had to do was pay the other £800,000. Maurice Johnston might well have taken them to court and he might have won but the most important thing was that Celtic would not have been embarrassed.

'I warned them of Rangers' interest because although it wasn't mentioned openly people knew about it. And the directors knew about it. I was on holiday in America and I had already told Andy Roxburgh that this fella might not be available for his World Cup qualifiers because he might be sitting in the stand when I heard that Celtic had issued a statement saying that as a matter of principle Johnston was free to go.

'I said, "Aw, in the name of God, there's only one place he can be going." I knew the effect of it. We never recovered. I'm not shouldering the blame for that because as far as I'm concerned he was our player. It was Maurice Johnston who got in touch with me saying he wanted to come to Celtic. He came chasing us and from then on it went downhill.

'I'll tell you one thing – it's very seldom you get a board of directors who want to face the flak. The manager will always go first, because it's certainly not going to be them. I went, fine . . . but they went as well.

'When I look back and think of the traumas you create for your partner as a manager, it's a wonder they can stay married to you. When I left Celtic I thought life was coming to an end but four or five months down the road you discover that this life isn't so bad. I'm still very much bound up in Celtic's future, I still very much want them to do well, but I'm not going to jump off a cliff if things don't work out the way I would like.

'And I do have those memories. When you look back on it, financially we just weren't in the same ocean as the modern players. But having said that, few of them will experience the sheer number of wonderful afternoons and nights that came our way and if any player nowadays were to be fortunate enough to be part of such an occasion as we were in that last match of '78–'79, I guarantee this . . . they will never, ever surpass it.'

Billy McNeill underwent a triple bypass heart operation in March 1997. A month later he was back in action and was able to travel with the Scottish squad for their World Cup qualifying meeting with Belarus in Minsk as a member of the BBC Scotland commentary team.

Davie Hay

CELTIC 2 LEEDS UNITED 1

15 April 1970

EVEN in a sport which habitually exaggerates its own importance there is room for images of true enormity. Almost 30 years after it took place, the meeting of Celtic and Leeds United in the semi-finals of the European Cup can be described as a colossal event. It may be that somewhere in Europe a football crowd will one day exceed the assembly of 136,505 spectators who gathered at Hampden Park on the evening of 15 April 1970 to witness a contest between the champions of Scotland and England, but is a sure bet that it will not happen in Scotland. The combined capacities of Celtic Park, Ibrox and Hampden would be required to cope with what is now an almost unimaginable multitude.

Another certainty is that the official attendance given for that spring evening is not correct. The print run of tickets was limited to 134,000 and they sold out while the ink was still wet. A thriving trade in forgeries was established in Glasgow pubs and even that illegal supply could not satisfy demand. On the night of the game desperate supporters tried the usual direct methods – scaling the Hampden walls, throwing themselves over the turnstiles or slipping the operators a couple of quid to let them double up with a mate – and even then the seething weight of numbers outside caused a gate to be broken down.

The authorities simply stopped counting at 136,505. The true attendance could have been anything up to 145,000. The world record is 200,000 at the Maracana in Rio but the Brazilians built that stadium deliberately to exceed Hampden and they guaranteed the crowd by giving away free tickets. If Celtic had been distributing tickets for nothing they would have had to build a couple of Maracanas to cope with the people who wanted to be there for the Leeds game. This is the fixture which holds the record for any European tie, including finals. It was also the greatest attendance for any game in Britain not played on a Saturday.

The main reason for the match fever was that Celtic were favourites after winning the first leg 1–0 at Elland Road by a George Connelly goal. That itself had been a facer for the many English commentators who had billed the tie as the Battle of Britain – a label which was used again in 1992 when Rangers met Leeds in the second round of the same tournament – and even Match of the Century.

True, Celtic had been the first British team to win the European Cup only three years previously, opening the door for Matt Busby's Manchester United the following season, but the reigning champions of Scotland and England had never met in a Uefa competition and the usual southern conceits were quickly paraded, so much so that Jock Stein was even prepared to warn the English press of the hazards of their own prognosis when he said: 'We find ourselves in an unusual position because usually we're favourites. We're not favourites tomorrow and that, gentlemen, does not bother us at all. Even people who are well disposed towards us think Leeds will beat us. We'll soon see, won't we?'

Stein, whose credentials were not exactly required for inspection, was matching wits with Don Revie, the Leeds manager who, like his Celtic counterpart, would go on to take charge of his national team. Revie, whose name was synonymous with gamesmanship, had started to prepare the ground by saying that his team had been worn down by the demands of progressing through the FA Cup and defending their championship in what the English press liked to call the greatest league in the world. There was some truth in this but by implication – and sometimes by open accusation – Celtic were playing in a backwater.

Certainly the record of English clubs in Europe in the previous ten years was impressive. Manchester United, Tottenham Hotspur, West Ham United, Liverpool, Birmingham City, Newcastle United and Leeds had reached a total of eight European finals, with a record of five wins and three defeats. The Scottish showing was not exactly insubstantial, however. Celtic's European Cup win was the pinnacle, of course, but Rangers had made it to two Cup Winners Cup finals and between them, the Old Firm,

Charlie Nicholas

RIGHT: Davie Provan

FAR RIGHT: Murdo MacLeod

BELOW: Roy Aitken

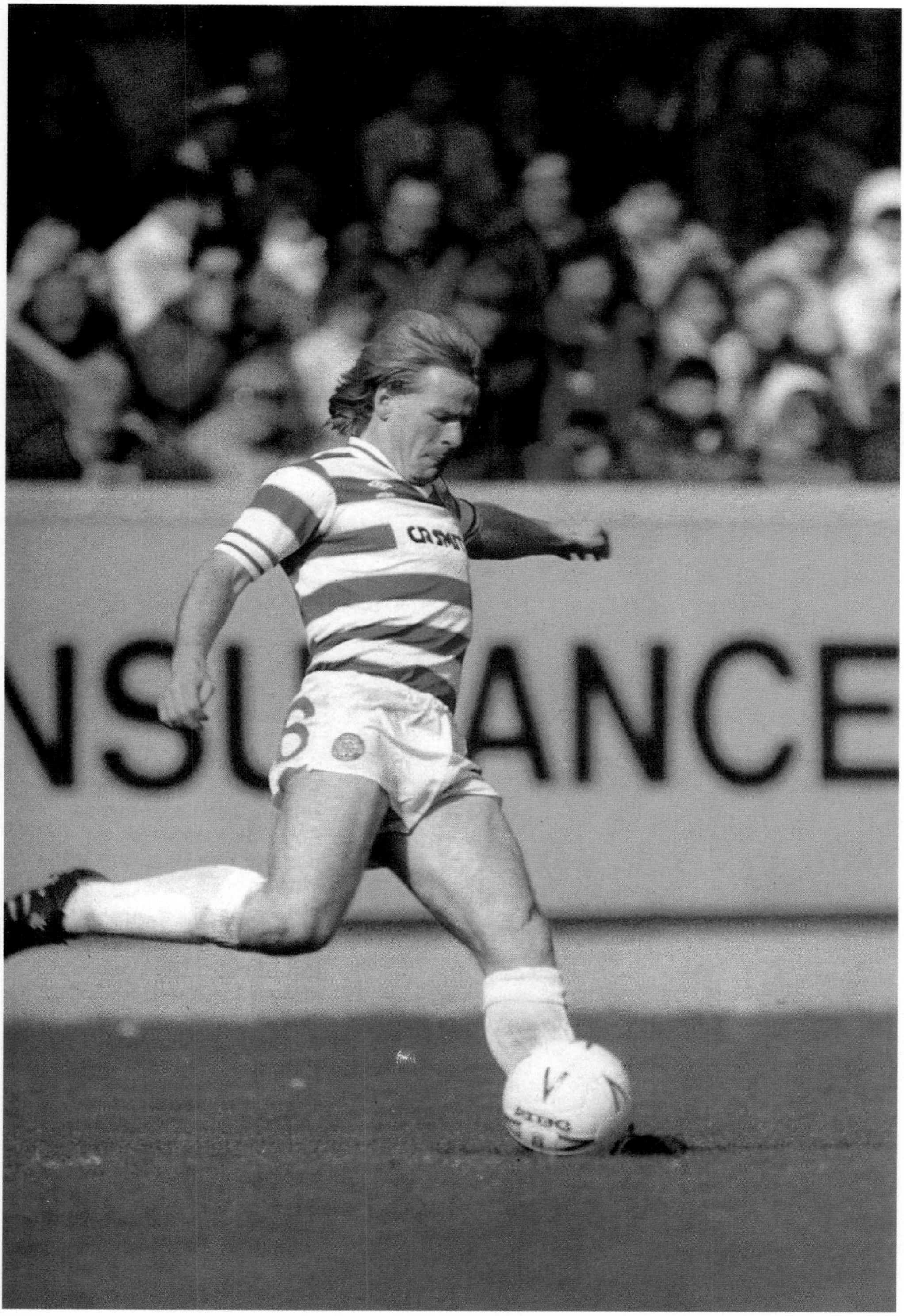

NSU ANCE

ABOVE: Packie Bonner

LEFT: Billy McNeill

ABOVE: Davie Hay (left)
RIGHT: Danny McGrain

Peter Grant

ABOVE: Tommy Burns
LEFT: Paul McStay

Jim Craig

Dundee, Dunfermline and Kilmarnock had been semi-finalists in the three European tournaments six times. Scotland should be such a backwater nowadays.

In any case, Celtic, too, were defending their title and pursuing a league and cup double which would culminate in a Hampden final against Aberdeen. Stein, wise to Revie's manoeuvrings, dismissed suggestions of fatigue because he knew that although Leeds had to cope with a backlog of fixtures, their manager had rejected opportunities to work through postponed ties. Revie had also clearly decided upon his priorities because he had fielded half a reserve side on the previous Saturday and the entire second string in a league match at Derby on the Monday, two days before the visit of Celtic, a circumstance which would never be sanctioned nowadays.

What was more to the point as far as Stein was concerned was that Leeds had genuine strength and quality in abundance. The side was almost a British Isles select, with Scottish internationals like Billy Bremner, Eddie Gray and Peter Lorimer, Johnny Giles, the guileful Republic of Ireland midfield star and a Welsh goalkeeper in Gary Sprake.

Then there was a contingent which doubled up for England, in which Jack Charlton was foremost amongst players like Terry Cooper, Paul Madeley, Allan Clarke, Norman Hunter, Mick Jones and Paul Reaney. Even at this distance, Celtic supporters who remember those names will readily concede that Leeds United were exceptionally formidable opponents. Hunter, known as 'Bite Yer Legs', was injured and missed the tie with Madeley replacing him in midfield.

Celtic, though, were also a side with impressive pedigree and it seems astonishing that players of the calibre of Tommy Gemmell, Bobby Murdoch, Billy McNeill, Jimmy Johnstone, Bobby Lennox, George Connelly, Willie Wallace and Bertie Auld could be lightly ranked as underdogs – but they were. There was also a young man who had cost Celtic the princely sum of two footballs, handed over to St Mirren's Boys' Guild when he was signed from them by Sean Fallon in 1965.

Davie Hay was the second of the clutch of remarkably gifted youngsters – nicknamed the Quality Street Gang – to become established as successors to the Lisbon Lions. George Connelly graduated to the first team in 1968–69 and Hay a year later. Hay was a double asset for Celtic because it was quickly apparent that not only was he a class player, he was also versatile. Stein noted early that the youth's easy-going habits masked a stubborn will and a deeply competitive nature and by the time Celtic prepared to face Leeds at Elland Road the manager knew he could hang his hat on Hay's imperturbability, despite the intensity of the occasion and the fact that his full back had yet to win a cap for Scotland (although that was about to be rectified).

As for Hay, he was already an admirer of his manager's meticulous ways. 'The very fact that it was a European Cup semi-final meant that there would be a lot of hype regardless of who we played. Once we knew it was Celtic v. Leeds we were immediately into the Scotland v. England rivalry and the publicity went through the roof but when you're a player you very often don't read the papers the way the fans do and if you get hyped up it's because of the way your manager motivates you, how he plans the game and puts across your chances of winning.

'We were up for the game, all right. It was a short journey down to Yorkshire and there were thousands of Celtic fans travelling down at the same time as us, so we knew we would have a sizeable support at Elland Road and that we were in for a very big night. We went down on the Monday by train to stay in Harrogate and then trained at Elland Road the following evening.

'Me and George Connelly were great pals and we were room-mates and I do remember that night that ourselves and Lou Macari, maybe because we had been resting for most of the day, weren't very tired. So we sat up playing cards into the morning, till about one or two o'clock in our rooms, which was maybe not exactly what Jock had in mind for us but we wouldn't have got to sleep otherwise.

'On the way to the game itself we really started to pick up the atmosphere because there were so many Celtic fans around and the noise and the colour inside Elland Road was amazing. Most people will know the story about our stockings. About half an hour before the game we were told we would have to change our stockings because ours were white like Leeds'. Those were the days when clubs didn't have umpteen sets of away strips like they use now, for commercial reasons as well as the obvious ones, and nobody had suggested before we travelled that we would have to switch colours.

'So Leeds offered us the choice – of orange stockings or blue stockings. We chose orange but, strangely enough, if we needed any little final motivation, that was it. In fact, we played so well that night that we talked about playing the second leg with the same stockings, but we never carried that one through. The other point which Jock stressed in the dressing-room was that Jimmy Johnstone could be the match winner and he got the wee man going so much that he played one of the best games of his career that night.

'Something else which had an effect on us was the warm-up before the game. As you know, it's automatic now that players go out on the pitch for their warm-up but we never did that prior to normal league or cup games at home. In Europe it was all part of the hype to get players out on the field. It was a tradition but also it was sensible if you were playing on an unfamiliar pitch. That night it gave us a feel for the atmosphere of the game and the Celtic fans were in full voice over on the right-hand side as we came out of the tunnel.

'They might not have made up half of the crowd but it couldn't have been too far away from that and mostly they were behind the goal where we actually scored. The Leeds fans were trying to compete with them before the game but once we went ahead I could only really hear our supporters, so I suppose it must have been a strange one for the Leeds players on their own ground.'

An odd coincidence links Celtic's visit to Elland Road in 1970 with Rangers' European Cup-tie there 23 years later. In both cases the Scottish champions scored in the opening moments and forced Leeds to chase the game. Against both Old Firm sides, too, Leeds scored the opening goal in Glasgow only to lose by the same margin in each case.

That Revie's men were shocked by such a swift collapse of all his disruptive strategies was not in doubt. The game was televised live in Scotland and hardly had the viewers noted that Celtic were wearing peculiarly tinted stockings – although on black and white television the effect was somewhat diminished – than they were leaping out of armchairs to celebrate George Connelly's opener.

The unfortunate Madeley took most of the blame for Celtic's goal. He might have cut out the danger on the right but he badly mistimed his challenge on Jimmy Johnstone and before the Englishman could recover the ball was swept across the face of the goal where Connelly struck a drive which deflected off Terry Cooper and spun past Sprake. Cooper spent much of the rest of the game being tormented by Johnstone, who had been wound up like a spring by the wily Stein; it was to be a hard evening for the Leeds full backs.

Whether because, as Revie would insist afterwards, his players were genuinely drained or whether they had found their momentum disrupted by his decision to leave them out in the preceding fixtures, Leeds looked flat. Connelly had the combative Giles in his pocket in midfield and Leeds began increasingly to depend upon high balls into the Celtic box, most of which were comfortably tidied away by Billy McNeill.

Billy Bremner was taken off suffering from concussion midway through the second half, although some observers noted caustically afterwards that several of his team-mates had sustained the same damage when Connelly put the ball in their net. Stein's orders were to attack at all opportunities and Celtic followed his guidance so completely in letter and spirit that the only scare around their own area was when Evan Williams flapped at a cross and was the subject of a furious tirade from Tommy Gemmell.

Meanwhile, at the other end of the field Sprake was in full acrobatic action as he was peppered with shots, particularly from Willie Wallace. Nor did Leeds get much respite from their half-time break because Celtic sprung the same unpleasant surprise on them almost as soon as the game had started again when wee Jinky set off on another slalom run through static opponents to finish with a pass to Connelly who again thrashed the ball home. It was ruled out for offside by the French referee whose decision was declared dodgy even by the home supporters.

It took well into the second half for Williams to make a real save, a brave dive at Allan Clarke's feet and although Eddie Gray hit the bar late in the game after a clever run and drive, it was Johnstone's show. Even when he had to drop back to his own penalty area to collect the ball, he was able to shrug past opponent after opponent on his upfield meanderings. Terry Cooper, who was used to getting forward for Leeds, hardly ever dared make an overlapping run.

'I felt it was a reasonably evenly contested match at Elland Road,' Hay recollects. 'But we had done the really vital part by scoring so early and I think that the lift we got from that and the blow they must have felt when George got his goal probably kept the game in our favour down there.'

Celtic held on to their lead with little concern and their fans capered through the Yorkshire night. Many of them even made it home in time for the replay. Not even Jock Stein could now suggest that his players were underdogs as ticket fever became a Glasgow pandemic.

'The first game was very special but the second leg was absolutely phenomenal,' says Hay. 'Everybody you met was looking for tickets for the second leg, so who knows how many people they could have got into Hampden if there had been enough space?

'Funnily enough, although we knew that we would be playing in front of a record crowd because of the number of tickets which were printed, you couldn't tell from the pitch because it wasn't always easy at Hampden to see the extent of the crowds. You know what it was like at night games, where it was quite often misty and there was always the cigarette smoke and the steam from people's breaths drifting up round the floodlights.

'So the crowd becomes a mass rather than 136,000 faces and I didn't look upon it as being frightening. I thought it was uplifting. I don't know if Leeds thought about it that way although their Scottish lads and some of the England players would certainly have seen it before and known what to expect. We did hear something about the forgeries and about the gate being broken down so, again, that let us know that we were in for a phenomenal evening but Jock made us concentrate on the jobs we had to do.

'What I did notice was that as far as you could see all round the ground it was only Celtic supporters. I didn't think Leeds had any fans with them although I've often thought since then that they must have done. I mean, they were a big club at the time and I can't believe their fans just gave up on the idea of travelling to Glasgow. But if they did, to this day, I've never heard from any of them. There was no segregation that night so if there were any Leeds supporters they would have been in with our fans, but they weren't making a song and dance about it.

'So, really, as far as we were concerned we had the entire crowd behind us. Jock might have been happier if Leeds had brought enough people to make a noise, I don't know. He was worried about complacency, that maybe we had got the idea that because we had won down in England it would be easier in Scotland and that maybe the crowd thought so, too. He thought Leeds would have a right go at us and he was right.'

Revie and his players had begun to sense that their whole season might end barren and that if they were to prevent such a draining anti-climax to their efforts on three fronts, they had reached the crucial moment. On the previous Saturday they had played Chelsea in the FA Cup final at Wembley, a game which ended in a 2–2 draw after extra time. If they were to confound Celtic it was absolutely essential that they take the lead and wipe out the advantage of the away goal scored by Connelly.

And, just as Celtic had ambushed them in the opening minutes at Elland Road to set themselves up for the rest of the night, so Leeds attempted to draw the Scottish champions into a tactical trap.

'In the first leg I played right back and Tommy Gemmell was at left back. At the start of the second leg they actually switched their wingers. Peter Lorimer went to outside left and Eddie Gray to outside right, which was not normal for them. I remember Tommy Gemmell shouting to the bench, 'Do you want us to change, boss?'

'But Big Jock felt that the reason for them doing that was to make us lose our shape, especially I think down the right side because I had developed a good relationship with Bobby Murdoch and wee Jimmy. So Big Jock told us to keep it the way it was and within five minutes Gray and Lorimer had reverted to their normal roles.

'I thought Hampden was made for us to play on that night. It was in good condition and we liked playing there. We didn't have a failing in the side. You go through from Evan, Tommy, Billy, Jim Brogan, Bertie, Bobby Murdoch, wee Jimmy – who was in another of his amazing moods – John Hughes, wee Bobby, everybody played to the top of their form.'

Yet it was Leeds United who scored first, with a marvellously conjured goal from Bremner, who was driving his team tigerishly from his beat in midfield and engaging in a mighty personal contest with Bertie Auld. Fourteen minutes into the game, with Celtic having enjoyed most of the pressure, the little red-headed man from Stirling accepted a pass from Hunter, pushed on until Williams' goal came within range and from 25 yards or so thrashed a breathtaking shot high past the keeper into the top corner of the net right in front of the cliffs of faces at the Celtic end.

Now, after Celtic's splendid efforts at Elland Road, the tie was all square and their away goal counted for nothing. Davie Hay was not perturbed.

'We just centred it and got on with the game. The attitude was, well, they've scored, it's a bit of a hiccup. There was no blame on anyone because it was a brilliant goal, great strike – but then Billy was an exceptional player.

'Even then, we didn't feel too perturbed. We had a game plan and we felt it was working and there was never, at any time, a sense that this game was running away from us at all, even when we were 1–0 down. There was just an inner belief that this was going to be one of our nights. We probably dominated the game at Hampden more than we had at Elland Road. Down there I felt it was fairly even but at Hampden we dominated for vast periods at a time.

'And we pressed them and went on pressing them and although we were still trailing at half-time, Jock told us that if we just kept doing what we had been doing, we would go on and win the game. He was right, as usual. He wanted to keep it fast and play it wide and that's how both our goals came about, from wide cutbacks. He said that the most important thing was to do everything quickly.'

Stein's insistence that Celtic would play their game their way imposed itself on Leeds. It also communicated itself to the ocean of supporters around the ground. This was perhaps the most evocative evening of all the old stadium's many theatrical nights. To stand on the terracings that evening and survey the stunning sweep of faces was a truly thrilling experience which has remained etched in the memories of everyone who was present. Not that most people enjoyed anything approaching comfort.

Towards the back of the standing areas at both ends and in the North Enclosure there was hardly an atom of space. The act of reaching down into a coat pocket to extract a can of beer and convey it to the lips required the contortionist skills of Houdini. Fans who had been unwise enough to lodge their carry-out bags between their feet had to endure a thirst which was made even more tormenting by the knowledge that the bevvy was so very close and quite impossible to reach. Some despaired as they felt the crucial supplies slither off down the steep slopes. Others stood on their cans to get a better view. The top half of the terracings was so tightly packed there was no possibility even of a sway.

Towards the front it was just possible to breathe in and out without becoming intimate with the next spectator. When Bremner scored there was a silence so complete that the Leeds players could be heard congratulating each other in the eerie vacuum of noise. Then, after 15 or 20 seconds the anthems started, louder even than the roar which had greeted the teams when they emerged from the tunnel. As each chorus faded at one end, the sound of 40,000 voices bellowing from the sides washed across the park until they too gave way to a more vague thunder of song from the masses half-hidden by the smoky mist behind the goal at the other end of the park. Nothing remotely like it had ever been seen or heard at any night game played in Britain and it is hard to imagine that it ever will again.

Faced with such a majestic demonstration of unity of will between the Celtic players and supporters, Leeds must be accorded great credit for keeping the issue in balance as long as they did. When eventually they were crushed, theirs was no disgrace. Leeds' centre forward, Mick Jones, was carried off with a nasty gash in his leg but he courageously took up his position again at the start of the second half. The green tide could not, however, be halted and it began to flood over the English champions within a couple of minutes of the restart.

'I think it was a case of us and the fans doing everything together that night. OK, we lost a goal and for a few seconds they're wondering what it's all about, but we automatically went forward again so we were in unison, whether you think that us attacking lifted the crowd, or having them behind us drove us on again. That ten seconds after Billy's goal was probably the only quiet time around Hampden for five or six hours that evening.

'Most of the rest of the game we had the crowd celebrating. We scored early in the second half from a short corner which I played to Bertie and he crossed into the box. It was a quality cross, a curler which was aimed for John Hughes and big Yogi launched himself at it for a header which was straight into the net. That was it, really, because we were ahead again and we were always going to win.

'None of us had ever, at any point in the game, thought we would lose it but now it was certain we would get a victory because we really were playing very, very well. And it was a hard game because they had people who could dig and so did we. I think that was the case in every area. Mind you, they don't dig harder than wee Bertie and although I missed it, I'm sure it was him who caught Mick Jones with a dull one.

'That was in the days when they didn't have massive numbers of cameras about the place. I'm not saying he did anything wrong, Bertie, but . . .

'So you had that one from Bertie but then they were no angels, you know, Bremner and Giles and Hunter and such like. There were a lot of men playing on both sides who, if required, could look after themselves. But it wasn't a physical type of game, it was a match played with very great ability and at an exceptional pace. That was a strength of Celtic's which was sometimes overlooked, that we could play to a high standard and at a very fast pace at the same time.

'There wasn't a lot of so-called banter as such. I think that was because there was a lot of respect between the two sides. There was the odd bit of talk. When Jones got injured there was something said. I remember Les Cocker, their trainer, coming on to treat him and he had a few words to say to Bertie, but Bertie in his usual fashion said, 'Well, we're all men out here', or something to that effect.

'But there wasn't any of the kind of talk that's meant to get something going by saying the wrong thing. We really did respect each other as men, as footballers and there was no need to have had that dimension to it. Everybody on both sides wanted to play – and could play.

'There was some wonderful wing play in that game, again on both sides. We had Jimmy Johnstone and because we were playing with three up the front John Hughes would be more through the middle but still powerful and very tricky for their defenders. And they had Lorimer and Gray – different styles but on their day very threatening wingers.

'I keep coming back to Jimmy, though, because I was well placed to watch him operating and as I say, he was phenomenal. You might argue about what was his best game ever but that night against Leeds would have to be up there at the top, maybe along with his performances against Red Star Belgrade the year before. You had to be on top of your game defensively if you were up against people like that plus, of course, the full backs were expected to overlap and you couldn't allow any of the wingers any amount of space.

'We're talking about wingers but whenever I look at the line-ups, it's really an astonishing amount of ability in just about every position on both sides and although the teams had different styles we were each great to watch when we were playing full out, so with the two sides really going at each other it had to be a classic game.

'Another of our particular strengths was that while we could move the ball about well and at a fast tempo the team was full of players who really knew the game and could make their moves off the ball and who were prepared to work very hard. Taking all that into account, I think that when Yogi scored just after half-time that was the game over in Leeds' eyes. I'm sure if you had asked them they would have said they knew at that moment that this was Celtic's night.

'Although I said I had felt that earlier even when they scored, this was the point when they knew they were out. I may be wrong if you were to go back and look at it move by move but my feeling was that they never really threatened us after that. It didn't help them when they lost their goalkeeper. Gary Sprake got into a collision with John Hughes and they had to take him off and bring on David Harvey, who started playing for Scotland not long after that.

'I think Harvey's first touch was to pick the ball out of his net. In fact, I'm sure of it because he was hardly on the field when we scored again. It was wee Jimmy who started it with one of his dribbles and he looked as if he was going to put in a cross – Leeds semed to believe that's what he was trying to do – but he remembered what Jock had said at half-time and he pulled the ball back for Bobby Murdoch who got a good hard shot in towards the corner of the goal. There wasn't much Harvey could do to stop it and he might have been unsighted by one of their players, anyway.

'It was only a matter of time before we were ahead on the night because even when we had been a goal down they had had to clear the ball off the goal line. Madeley and Cooper saved them a couple of times. After we scored the second goal Bertie Auld, Bobby Murdoch and George Connelly were running the show in midfield.

'We kept going. Even though the game was won 2–1 I don't think we could help attacking, although that might be deemed as an error. I don't think it was. I think the occasion geared us to do that. Sure, we gave it to wee Jimmy a bit more so he could take it for an extra dribble or two but we were after a third one. Of course, by now the fans were really enjoying themselves because they knew as well as anybody when we got the equaliser that we were never going to lose this game. This was why they had been going daft for tickets and we hadn't let them down, we had given them what they hoped for.

'But even when we were really well ahead in the game and we knew that Leeds weren't going to damage us, the play was still so fast that you had to have all your concentration on what was happening out on the pitch. I couldn't really look at what was happening up on the terracings until after the final whistle. I swapped shirts with Billy Bremner and we did our lap of honour.

'Unfortunately for us, that's when I think we probably fell into a trap. This game had been built up so much that people were calling it the final before the final so when we saw who we had to play next, we weren't really worried. We knew all about Leeds United and what a powerful team they were and we had beaten them home and away.

'Feyenoord were an unknown quantity. I saw an interview with Wim van Hanegem recently and he said that they expected, having watched our games with Leeds, that they would do well to keep the score down. We totally underestimated them, everybody at Celtic Park. I would never point the finger at Big Jock but he didn't really rate them as they should have been rated. And the irony is that he didn't put out the same team as he did against Leeds, which I think had a bearing on what happened.

'We changed our formation and played a 4–4–2 instead of 4–3–3. Strangely enough we played poorly that night and we almost got away with beating them.'

Perhaps because of the romance of Lisbon three years previously and the sheer scale of the events at Hampden Park, Celtic had lost their sense of wonder and in Milan they allowed Feyenoord to emerge from behind their awe after a dull first half. The Dutch played a version of the Italian *catenaccio* defence which Celtic had so decisively shredded against Inter in Lisbon three years previously, but they supplemented it with the desire and ability to attack with menace when the opportunity was offered.

Even so, with Jimmy Johnstone a wan imitation of the destroyer of the Leeds defence, and playing well below their habitual pace, Celtic took the lead when Gemmell accepted a free kick from Murdoch on the edge of the box and smashed it into the net as he had done for his goal in Lisbon. Then Celtic fell into a stupor and allowed Israel to score with a simple unchallenged header. Feyenoord hit the post but Celtic survived to drag the game into extra time.

'They outplayed us and we knew it. They hit the post and even then we still couldn't lift ourselves but in extra time we could have won it almost right away because John Hughes robbed one of their guys and he was right in on goal but their goalkeeper made a good save. If that had gone in I think we would have won.

'It was still level when we got to half-time of extra time. Then a couple of minutes after we turned around, Ove Kindvall had a shot which came off Evan Williams' feet. They scored the winner almost at the end. Billy McNeill slipped when he was going for a through ball and he handled the ball in the box but the referee played advantage because Kindvall was on to it and he scored.

'In those days there were no penalty kick deciders and I have always felt that if we had held out and got a replay we would have beaten them. You can never be sure it would have been different and they totally deserved their win on the night but I don't believe we would have played like that two games in a row. It was a great lesson in how if you go in expecting to win in football, you can get the big custard pie in the face.'

Hay played for another four years for Celtic, recording a total of over 220 appearances before he left for Chelsea in 1974, after excellent displays for Scotland in the World Cup finals in West Germany. His departure was not popular with the fans and it would have been less so had they known how inferior Celtic were to Chelsea in one department.

'I wanted a higher basic wage, more like the money I could earn in England. Celtic's argument was that my *salary* was comparable but that was only true if you got to the European Cup final, won the league and the Scottish Cup and earned the bonuses. I made the decision to go when I didn't want to leave Celtic but my basic wage here was £65 and when I went to Chelsea it was £215. Plus there were other enticements at Stamford Bridge.

'Fortunately, that's all changed now. Souness started with Rangers so he could entice players from England but Celtic are in that bracket as well. If you want the best players, you have to pay the money. That was a lesson Celtic took a very long time to learn. They thought they were saving the club money and in the end it cost them a lot more than they would have had to spend.'

It was as well for Hay that at Stamford Bridge the remuneration was healthy because he found himself beset by injuries and ailments. He underwent five operations, including two on his eye, and he was ultimately forced to retire from playing in September 1979 as a result of a detached retina.

He stayed at Stamford Bridge to coach the youth team, was invited to become assistant manager of Motherwell under Ally McLeod and succeeded the former Scotland manager in 1981. The following year Motherwell won the first division championship, unbeaten at home.

Hay was invited to become Celtic manager in succession to Billy McNeill in July 1983. He guided the team to the championship in 1986, a League Cup final and two Scottish Cup finals, the second of which saw Celtic take the trophy in 1985 (*see Roy Aitken's chapter*). When Souness won the championship in his first season with Rangers in 1987, the board believed that Hay was not the charismatic personality required to go head to head with the new regime at Ibrox. He was invited to resign, refused and became the first Celtic manager to be dismissed.

But he had the last laugh, returning to Celtic Park after the revolution which displaced the men who had sacked him and he is now a valued member of the backroom staff, scouting for the club.

'I was bitter after they sacked me. I admit that. It was the manner in which they did it which angered me. OK, they had to go and get somebody else once they had decided I was going but I have always been basically a straight and honest guy and if they had been up front with me I would have been hurt, but not bitter. The irony is that now I'm back here and they've gone.

'I look back at the days when we could take on a team like Leeds and beat them home and away in a European Cup semi-final and I wish we had realised that those times don't last forever. Maybe a lot of people connected with the club thought that it would just go on and on, which it doesn't, not for any football club.

'What encourages me now is that Celtic are building a stadium which is comparable with the very best, we can almost fill it just with the season ticket holders and we're bringing the right kind of players here. We're in the big bucks game now. For me the best aspect of all is that Tommy and Billy work extremely hard and they're always trying to learn.

'I would say that we are getting our style right once more, something like the way we played in the days of games like the Leeds matches. We have yet to make ourselves top dogs in Scotland again and success in Europe is further down the road, but you can only have dreams in modern football if you have realism, too. That's what we are nowadays, a realistic club. And that is why we can have our dreams back again.'

Danny McGrain

ST MIRREN 0 CELTIC 5

3 May 1986

REMINISCENCES with Danny McGrain are not so much a stroll down memory lane as an expedition into Hampton Court maze. Promising routes lead up cul de sacs but an innocuous half-turn in the conversation can just as surprisingly get straight to the heart of the puzzle. When we met to discuss this chapter in his comfortable home in Old Kilpatrick he volunteered that it was his birthday, but was vague about exactly how old he was (not an uncommon phenomenon, to be fair). Reference books were on hand to resolve the matter – it was eventually established that he was 46 – whereupon he declared that he had started counting backwards the year before in order to reduce the generation gap with his three daughters.

'So I'm actually 44. Maybe this is what they mean when they wish you many happy returns,' he said by way of explanation. The surreal side of the McGrain psyche surfaced several times during a couple of hours which were frequently hilarious and for a man who apologises for his hopeless sense of recall he managed to keep the tape recorder running longer than any other contributor to this book.

'Put it this way,' he said, 'I played in seven Cup finals but if you took everything I remember from each of them and added it up it wouldn't amount to half a game. It's maybe to do with concentrating so hard on the job in hand that everything else seemed to pass by.'

McGrain does, however, clearly recall the truly spectacular climax to the 1985–86 season at Love Street. There can be few who were in the crowd who could not help him with every detail of that melodramatic afternoon in Paisley, when Celtic ran up five goals in 53 minutes and then spent an excruciating half hour riveted to the reports coming in from Dens Park where Heart of Midlothian needed only to draw against Dundee to win their first championship since 1960.

When the title swung towards Celtic in a climactic few minutes of almost unbearable intensity, McGrain was about to experience the intoxication of spectacular victory for the last time in a career with Celtic which, when it came to an end the following season, would span 20 years. The length of his service at Celtic Park was made all the more remarkable by the amount of physical damage he sustained over two punishing decades. World-class is a description used far too readily but it was never an overstatement when it was applied to the durable McGrain.

As a defender he was no giant at 5ft 9ins but when he sent his 12-stone frame into a tackle he left a succession of opponents with the impression that they had been run over by a small battle tank. He was, as Charlie Nicholas and Packie Bonner testify elsewhere in this book, the definitive professional footballer.

And, had Rangers not been repelled when they discovered that his full name was Daniel Fergus McGrain, he would have been an Ibrox signing, as every Celtic supporter knows – or at least, they believe they do. McGrain has previously testified himself that a Rangers scout was dissuaded from further interest by what were presumed to be the Catholic associations of his name, but now he has another version of the legend, although he admits that his family affiliations were directed towards Govan.

'If I supported anybody as a boy it must have been Rangers because my Dad used to take me to see them. Whether you could say I supported them is really another question because I was going along between the ages of five and ten and I can't say I was really aware of who I was supporting although I would be enjoying the game, or shouting or playing with other guys the same age as me and not really watching the match.

'But I was educated at a Protestant school and brought up in a Protestant family so I suppose I had to follow Rangers like my dad. We only went to home games, we were never travelling supporters and it's so long ago I can't truthfully say whether I enjoyed it or not. I was a great admirer of Ian McMillan, who maybe stuck out because although he played the game a little slower than a lot of others he could pass the ball with greater accuracy than them.

'Jimmy Millar scored goals, Ralph Brand walked about like Ralph Brand and there was Jim Baxter, but the player I remember best is Davie Wilson because of his white hair. His hair stood out against those dark terracings and that dark place in a dark time which we all had to come through. *(Note – For readers aged less than thirtysomething, McGrain is referring to the austerity of the 1950s, a decade which now seems to have been populated by people wearing trenchcoats and smoking Woodbine in the drizzle.)*

'I didn't start playing football at school until I was ten because I went to Camus Place Primary in Drumchapel which had no pitches. The school did get an under-12 team together and we won some competition at the Maryhill Harp ground – black ash, a horrible, horrible place – and I don't remember anything about the game (surprise) but I do remember the cafe in Maryhill Road where we went for a celebratory ice cream.

'I still have the medal, a highly prized thing which is with all the rest of my medals – I don't know where they are. I went on to Kingsridge Secondary in Drumchapel, played for Scottish Schools and Sean Fallon was there. This is where I've got to correct the Rangers story. I'm sure that they had checked what school I went to before their scout came to look at me – it wouldn't have been hard to do in a schools team – but this story has got out of hand.

'I mean, If Daniel McGrain is a Catholic sounding name, then so be it, but in that case it must have sounded Catholic before the Rangers scout came to see me. However, somebody said it somewhere and now it's just one of those stories everybody thinks is true. Same as I'm supposed to hate English people because of some remark I made after I was playing for Scotland and England beat us.

'Certainly, I didn't like the England players for beating us but I wouldn't like Brazilian players if they beat us, either. I wasn't very sporting then, right enough. Anyway, to get back to the point, I was playing schools football in the morning and for Queen's Park in the afternoon. The first time I played England was at that time and we got hammered 4–0 at Ibrox. England were a team of giants and we were a typical, wee Scottish team, nothing over 5ft 8ins – except for the centre half who wasn't too good – and I got carried off with cramp because I was trying to impress the scouts who were there.

'Sean Fallon contacted my dad a few days later and I signed for Celtic part-time. This wasn't so good because, basically, I didn't want to work. I'd got four O-levels and that was me. I had no inclination to do anything although for some reason I had a fancy for mechanical engineering. Why, I do not know. So I went to Reid Kerr College in Paisley, travelling from Drumchapel into Clydebank, a bus along from there to the ferry, over the Clyde and another bus along to the college on five pounds a week wages from Parkhead.

'I look back now, as we all do, and ask where has it all gone? That time just sped past but it was hard because it's well-nigh impossible to work if you're not attuned to what you're doing. I did get my City & Guilds qualification after a year but Kenny Dalglish and I made a pact that we would go to Mr Stein together and threaten him if he didn't make us full-timers.

'I'd be 17 and Kenny would be a bit younger. The big thing we had to decide was who would go in first. If somebody wants to make a film of this book, what happened was this. I went in and I told Mr Stein, "Look, I'm a right good player and you're going to sign me and give me five grand a week. Kenny's all right, so you take a chance on him, even if he's no' as good as he thinks he is."'

'But back in the real world, that was the hardest thing I've ever done in football, to ask Mr Stein to go full-time. To play football is easy. It came naturally, playing for a good team in which so much was done for you off the ball. To go and ask Mr Stein who was a giant of a person, a mega man and somebody we had hardly ever actually seen, was something else. And he must have seen something he liked about us because he agreed and I played with Kenny Dalglish continuously for three years.

'We asked Mr Stein. He didn't ask us. If we hadn't done that I would have been a mechanical engineer and Kenny would have been a joiner, thoroughly enjoying himself – because I'm sure he's not enjoying himself now. Celtic farmed me out to Maryhill Juniors at Lochburn Park and I have no fond memories of that at all.

'I remember the damp dressing-rooms, I remember the road up to it which was very handy for the pubs – some of the players seemed to go down there at half-time for about half an hour – but my most delightful memory is of my first game. At half-time they were lighting up the fags, somebody was passing round a can of lager and I said to myself, "I think I'm here to learn, or toughen up or whatever. Do I take a swig of the lager and a puff of the cigarette?"

'Thankfully, I didn't. I was there for six months and didn't win a single game. I remember Paul Wilson coming to join us from

Cumbernauld or somewhere and I saw him being tackled and hit so hard that he ended up on the terracing. The games were insignificant because nothing really happened. I played left midfield but what I learned I do not know. I'm not actually decrying it because I maybe discovered what it is like to be defeated and appreciate the feelings of players who lose.

'Defeat is bitter and not a pleasant experience. I knew that after I left Maryhill Juniors although there were guys there, playing away and enjoying themselves. Great, there's something for everybody, but I went back to Celtic knowing I never wanted to lose again. I'm not saying it made me a winner but after that, if I was beaten by a better player at golf or a better team at football, I knew I had to try harder or be beaten again.'

It was a sentiment which governed McGrain's career completely and sustained him through a catalogue of setbacks so severe that it was almost ridiculous that he should have survived – and survived repeatedly to stay at the top until he was 38, which is into the dotage of the average British player.

First came the fractured skull at Brockville in 1972.

'That happened when I was playing against an old adversary of mine, Dougie Somner. Now Dougie is a great guy – as we all are – but when it comes to putting on the boots and strip we tend to be nasty people. It's a professional game, you're there to win for yourself and your team and some mild-mannered people actually turn vicious. I'm not saying that about Dougie, mind you, but he was as committed as I was.

'We both went for a header, he was just a fraction late and we clashed heads. How many times does that happen and the players just pick themselves up? Maybe there's a bit of blood but that's it. I was blacked out. Neil Mochan stuffed smelling salts up my nose and people who have gone through that will know that smelling salts could put the head of an elephant back on its shoulders. At half-time I got the sponge, the ice and a cup of tea.

'Lou Macari said to me, 'On you go, you'll be all right.' Wee Lou was a substitute and he didn't want to play because it was a right cold day. Like all butch football players I said, yeah, OK, although I didn't feel fine, but I thought that I would probably be all right once I got out into the fresh air. I got to the door and the next thing I knew I was in hospital.

'So I take it wee Lou had to go on.' (*He did. Celtic won 1–0 with a Vic Davidson goal.*)

After he left hospital and coped with the minor inconvenience of double vision which lasted three months McGrain started training again, using first balloons then soft balls and finally the regulation footballs to regain his heading ability.

'Naivety is a great saviour. I've found that the less I know the better off I am. If I had known then what I know now it might have held me back. I just put my trust in what people told me. In one of my first games back, against Aberdeen, for some reason I was either bending down or getting back to my feet when the ball hit me square, dab in the middle of my head and I went down.

'I thought, yes, I'm OK. The whole crowd went quiet. I should actually have played on it for the sympathy vote, but I just got up – and got a loud cheer for it – but again I had no idea what the consequences might have been.'

Having failed to stop McGrain in his tracks by what might be called the bludgeon method, fate came back with a more subtle strategy. In 1974 he was diagnosed as suffering from diabetes.

'Again I was very naive. I had no sportsman or woman to contact who had been through this in the same kind of circumstances as me, nobody who had such an active life as I did that I could ask for advice. So I just carried on myself with trial and error – fortunately not a lot of errors – but I should have known things about diabetes which would have made it easier to control.

'Never in any games I played in did I have any wanderings or stupor, which does happen – you do have hypos – and that's when people who know you have to be aware that you're diabetic and that the symptoms can cause you to stagger about like a drunk person. It's not hard for some diabetics to go into a coma. Comas are all right if you're caught within a certain amount of time but I never really had any serious problems.

'The difficulties would be maybe after a game, going for a meal at a restaurant where the service might be slow, which can be serious if you have taken your injection and the food doesn't arrive within half an hour so that you have a carbohydrate intake. That happened to me one night and I took a hypo but luckily my wife was there and got some sugar into me and I was fine. So that was the diabetes.'

By 1977 the gods of misfortune had worked out that even the apparently indestructible Danny McGrain could not continue to play football with only one serviceable foot. The damage was done on 1 October 1977, in a game against Hibernian at Easter Road.

Recollecting the malady which came closest to halting his career, McGrain paused like a wine connoisseur savouring a particularly fragrant vintage.

'Ah, the injury of '77 . . . one of the first games of the season. In the Hibs team was John Blackley, one of my best friends. I don't know what it is amongst football players but when you go into the tackle, if you're up against a pal you always go in harder. Maybe it's because you think he's going to do that to you so you have to make sure he feels it, too. For some reason, I found myself up around their 18-yard line and John, being the Hibs sweeper, was going to clear the ball so I went in, not dirty but determined to win the ball because I thought, if I win this tackle I can talk about it after the game. If he wins it, he'll dig me up about it.

'Both of us went into it more ferociously than we should have done. My ankle was sore but you get these knocks and grazes that don't do you any harm. I looked back and John was still lying on the ground. I went, "Oh, ya beauty. I won." So he got up and they gave him the sponge, nothing serious. He must have twisted his ankle. There's no way he was in serious agony or I wouldn't have left him lying there. So I knew I hadn't hurt him too badly – but I had hurt him enough.

'I had just come up to the halfway line and my ankle was getting sorer but I wasn't going to show to John that he had hurt me as well – stupidly, like the five-year-olds we all are. The following morning my foot was sore, as if I had stood on a stone, so I went in to see Bob Rooney. He said, "I think you've stood on a stone."

'I said, "If this is because I stood on a stone I've got a claim against the people who made my boots." Which shows you what I thought of that, because with the boots we had then if you stood on a rock you wouldn't feel it. Over the next few days the pain moved from the ball of my foot to the inside of the ankle, then to the outside of the ankle, then to my big toe. I couldn't go to a doctor or physiotherapist and ask them what was causing this because the following day or the day after the pain would be off somewhere else.

'So I went down to Manchester for a biopsy then to Oswestry in Wales where they looked at it with a machine which detected pain through the heat it was causing; the pain spots would vary. The guys who were looking at this were totally bemused at how this could be happening. I mean, I don't get anything simple like a broken leg. I've got to get something nobody can understand.

'In Manchester I saw a surgeon called Freddie Grifiths, who Mr Stein rated highly after he had had his car crash. He did the biopsy and basically, the bottom line was that nobody knew what was causing the trouble. I had letters from people telling me to bathe my foot in the Irish peat bogs, or to see faith healers and holy people.

'I didn't do anything except rely on my usual method of hoping things would just get better. Jim Steele, who used to be the Celtic masseur, went to a guy called Jan de Vries, who was an acupuncturist down in Troon. Steelie had a sore back or something and told me that Jan de Vries had worked well for him, so I thought, OK, I'll go and see him. At this point my foot wasn't as sore as it had been and it was healing.

'So I went with Jimmy Steele down to Jan de Vries and after the first session of these pins in my foot I thought, why am I letting this quack do this to me? But it wasn't sore next day. And another thing which did seem to work was that he said that he knew what it was and could treat it. I don't know if there and then I was cured, because I used to worry that it was something mental, but I don't think it could have been in the mind because the pain could be quite serious.

'Jan de Vries gave me that confidence in him and I went down for six months every Thursday night. Steelie would drive me down and I would have an hour of treatment. Jim Steele was my guardian angel at that time. And in the end it got better but to this day I still don't know what the trouble was. Even Jan de Vries never said exactly what he thought I had.'

For a third time, then, McGrain was able to achieve a comeback. This latest absence from the Celtic first team was prolonged and it took him 18 months to be restored to first team action. It was soon after this that Charlie Nicholas, as recounted elsewhere in these pages, noted the meticulous preparations undertaken by McGrain prior to each game. How much had the repeated physical disruption – especially the foot injury – depleted his strength and ability?

'Well, I wasn't the same player I had been, that's for sure. I couldn't get the same bite into my tackles and there wasn't much scope for the runs back and forward on the overlap. But you learn to compensate and find other things you can do comfortably. I don't think I was as conscientious as all that, but Charlie came through at a time when I was enjoying keeping fit, enjoying the company, enjoying the football.

'I'm sure I had depressing times and phases which got me down but I think Charlie kept me going because of his chirpiness, his cheekiness and his natural ability. When I saw him coming through it gave me a buzz, watching him progress, scoring goals from unlikely angles and playing with great natural ability. It wasn't just Charlie, it was the others who pushed on through into the team like Tommy Burns, Roy Aitken, Peter Grant and Paul McStay. Packie Bonner's first big game was my testimonial.

'Danny Crainie, Michael Conroy, Willie McStay – they were all of a breed who were cheeky and funny but prepared to work very, very hard, just as the Lisbon team had been cheeky and drunk an awful lot but devoted to working at their game. So both generations, and mine in between, worked extremely hard. Ability, the desire to win and having the support behind each generation enabled us to win and to find it all very enjoyable.

'To see these lads growing as people, as nice, honest guys as well as good players, gave me great pleasure because I was involved in helping them do that. Plus I was born fit, so it wasn't too hard for me, although the long stuff knackered me and as I got older it got longer and longer. It did my brains in, to be honest with you.'

No season was longer for McGrain than 1986–87. For one thing, he was 36 years old and very definitely in the twilight of his career and for another, Celtic had spent six months doggedly pursuing Hearts, the surprise league leaders, with little prospect of reward as the Edinburgh side put together an astounding sequence of 31 games without defeat, 27 of them in the championship.

Musing on the course of the league campaign a month before the end of the season the Celtic manager, Davie Hay, told the author: 'Hearts can be caught but we won't be able to drop any points or they'll get away from us. The thing which worries me most is that it's like the last few fences in the Grand National, when you're running out of chances that the front runners might make a mistake.'

Signs that the leading horse might be choking under the strain emerged towards the end of April. In the first Scottish league match to be televised live Hearts fell behind to Aberdeen at Tynecastle when Peter Weir scored with a penalty kick 15 minutes from time. With only three minutes left, however, the former Celtic winger, John Colqhoun beat Brian Gunn for an equaliser which kept Hearts three points ahead.

Hearts' next match was another home fixture, this time against Clydebank but the Edinburgh players were again nervy and it took a superbly struck drive from Gary Mackay to secure a 1–0 victory. Celtic meanwhile beat Dundee 2–0 and when Hay's side secured another two points with the same score against Motherwell in a postponed match at Fir Park the following Wednesday, Hearts began to regret their hesitancy against Clydebank.

Had they scored three or four goals against Clydebank Hearts would have been virtually invulnerable but as it stood on the last day of the league season their goal difference cushion was modest, only four goals superior to Celtic. They did, of course, have a two point lead so that they travelled to Dens Park knowing that a win or draw against Dundee would take the flag to Tynecastle. Even a defeat would not necessarily deprive them of the championship. If Hearts were to lose 1–0, Celtic would require a 3–0 victory over St Mirren to draw level on points and goal difference but take the title by virtue of greater number of goals scored.

Such paper calculations did not allow for another crucial factor, an ingredient which had not escaped McGrain's attention.

'Hearts had enjoyed a magnificent season but we had almost caught up with them and by taking it to the last game we had one advantage. We had been there before, not in such a tight situation, perhaps, but the players had experienced cup finals and big tense games so it was probably easier for us to bed into it than it would have been for Hearts.

'But I think, although we scored five goals, Davie Hay being the man he is has got to take a great deal of credit from it – which he has never got. Davie has never been given the credit he is due for what happened in that game. We were players, did our job. That's what we were paid for as was Davie, but he was so calm before the match that it had a great effect on the lot of us. Davie could be calm if the *Titanic* was sinking. I didn't realise at the time how cool he was, but then hindsight is a great teacher.

'If he had been hyped up and saying, we've got to score this and we've got to do that, it might have had the opposite effect on us. But he let us get on with it ourselves because he knew that it would be the best way, that we were quite capable of understanding what had to be done without somebody jumping up and down and getting us too excited.

'We were away to the races early on when Brian McClair got the first goal, which was a header from a corner kick from Owen

Archdeacon. Mo Johnston scored the second goal after a good pass from Paul McStay, as I remember, put him through on his own. We were really on top by then and we got the third goal right away. I started that move when I gave the ball to Murdo MacLeod.

'Then Paul McStay got it and he pushed it to Roy Aitken. By this time, I was up in their penalty area – which we will come back to – Roy passed to me and I gave it to Brian McClair. I think he nutmegged a St Mirren defender and then he cut it back right across the goal and Mo was in the right place to stick it away.

'The peculiar thing about that goal is that I know I started in our box and ended up in theirs but I can't remember how that happened. I do not know how I got there. I saw myself on television standing there with my hands up as Mo Johnston scored. I think I was taken away by spacemen. It might have been Dr Spock but somebody beamed me up and zoomed me to their 18-yard line.

'We knew that if we scored three we were definitely in with a chance but we could have been winning 55–0 and still lost the championship if Hearts weren't beaten at Dens Park. So the supporters were going wild but then they quietened down again. We scored again before half-time, a Paul McStay goal.

'And all the time Davie was Mister Calm, even at 3–0 and 4–0, because there was no news from Dundee. We went in at half time and he was just the same. Brian McClair got another goal in the second half and Davie never changed. But when I say he was Mister Calm, when the first goal was scored in Dundee all that calmness went straight out the window.

'He had taken me off by that time. I wasn't too pleased about it because I wanted to finish the game but I was perhaps tiring a little bit and Davie being the manager would have noticed that. I was telling you about being moved around the pitch by spacemen and I really felt that something like that had happened, that I was moving through the game robotically, machine-like, because I didn't feel tired. I don't think I looked tired but obviously I must have done for him to put me on the bench.

'So he put on Peter Grant and I was sitting at the side. I remember Davie suddenly being out on the track shouting that it was 1–0 to Dundee and I thought, now we can win this, we really can win this.

'After the game I really felt sorry for St Mirren because we could have played Inter Milan that day and beaten them 5–0 if that's what it would have taken to win the league. The players had not spoken about it very much. I was the captain but I hadn't been going about saying, right, let's beat this lot because we *might* win the championship. We all just thought, come on, we'll hammer St Mirren.

'And we didn't stop at that, we played them off the park. We played some terrific football. Mo Johnston that day was outstanding. When he was in that kind of form I was always very happy that I didn't have to play against him because he must have been a nightmare for any defender. He was such a busy little goal getter. That afternoon he was so wound up for the game, as was Brian McClair, who was another Mister Cool.

'If you had told Brian beforehand that we would absolutely have to go for it, he would have said, "Aye, aye, right." But as soon as the whistle went, maybe as soon as the first goal went in, you could see that these two were right on song and it went through the team. Everything we did was working for us. Passes that might have gone under your feet or over your feet and out of the park on another day, were landing just where they should have done. The whole game took on a life of its own for us.

'I've never experienced anything like it in my life, ever before. Every player on the park did their part exactly as they should have done. You might think I'm exaggerating but it was one of these occasions – and they don't happen very often – when I thought we couldn't have gone wrong if we had tried. You quite often get games when eight or nine players are doing very well and two or three not performing, but this was a complete team performance.

'So I felt sorry for St Mirren because they were up against all this and they must have known that there would be people afterwards who would decry them, say they didn't try a leg. I know some of them were Celtic supporters but you always find – and I'm sure Rangers would say the same – that when you play against people who support you, they try much harder.

'They have a point to prove and it could be that they're trying to show you that they're good enough to play for your team. But as I said before, it's nearly impossible to play against a side when everything on the pitch is going for them. And that was before we heard that Dundee had scored. Just imagine what it was like to be a St Mirren player when they were 5–0 down and fighting hard not to let us get any more goals.

'They've stopped us scoring for half an hour and then the loudest roar of the day comes from the crowd and it's nothing to do with what's going on at Love Street. Now all our hopes and maybes were coming true. We knew immediately what it was. It couldn't have been anything else, not unless the whole crowd had won the pools at the same time. We heard the roar – what a roar it was, too – and we knew it couldn't be Hearts scoring because if that had happened the whole place would have been groaning.'

At that precise moment – 4.33 p.m. – wildly contrasting scenes were taking place at three grounds separated by 90 miles but linked by the radio commentaries which were flashing between them. At Dens Park, the Hearts support watched in stupefaction as their team, weakened by a virus which had been kept secret from the press, literally slumped towards defeat. Robert Connor took a corner kick on the right, John Brown flicked it on and the unpoliced Albert Kidd struck a right-foot dive past Henry Smith from close range. There were seven minutes left to play and Hearts had conceded a goal from a corner for the first time that season.

Five miles from Paisley at Ibrox, a thin crowd of 21,500 were watching Rangers beat Motherwell 3–0, a victory necessary to keep Dundee at bay in the chase for the final Scottish place in the UEFA Cup. The Rangers fans had already decided it was better to be out of Europe than to qualify with Celtic taking the title. Hearing that a goal had been scored at Dens the Rangers supporters went wild, assuming that Walter Kidd had netted, only to be deflated abruptly as word spread that it was his namesake Albert who had earned the credit. Their hopes had been raised and squashed by a spectacular example of Kiddology.

And at Love Street, an utter frenzy of celebration erupted on the terracings. The bedlam had not let up at all when . . .

'We got the news that Dundee had scored again. Now we still had to be on our guard because if we had lost a goal and Hearts had got one back right away it could all still go wrong. St Mirren had gone, though, and I have no memory of them even coming near our goal.

'Then the final whistle went and it was a funny, funny feeling because at the beginning of the game you're hoping that you might win it, working out where we would be if this happened or that occurred – maybe the Hearts bus would break down on the way to the game and we'd get the title by default – but all of that went to the back of your mind and only came up when Dundee scored.

'Now that Hearts are losing, it's you that's under pressure. The big thought is don't lose this now, don't lose it. There's seven minutes to go and we can win this championship. OK, it's by goal difference but I don't care how you win it because it means you're in the European Cup next season. It was a terrible time for me sitting in the dugout because that's where you start to think, what if? When you're out on the field you're too busy to think.

'Then, as I say, the final whistle went and the players and the supporters went completely mental. I'm trying to describe the feeling and I can't. You truly had to have been there, to have been part of it, the whole crowd, the team and all. At that point I didn't quite know whether to feel sorry for the St Mirren players or thank them.

'I kept thinking that I had never experienced anything like this feeling. I certainly never experienced it again. It was 90 minutes of what – and it really is for lack of a better adjective, but it is absolutely true in this case – pure magic. We had spent part of the season languishing in a low position like second, something we did not like and we were determined to go out on a high so that as players we could not have been faulted.

'That day, how can I put it? If a knighthood had been presented for doing your best, every Celtic player would have got one. I won't say they were touched by God because I don't believe in God but something happened which was very extraordinary. I seemed to be floating. Honestly, I did. I was surrounded by joy. I was at the birth of my second daughter and I had a similar feeling, something you can't explain but you do experience.

'You know, we didn't even have any champagne with us in case we won. Or rather, some people didn't have champagne but Jimmy Steele did. (*Note – see also Charlie Nicholas's account of similar circumstances five years earlier.*)

'Jimmy had brought one or two bottles just in case. I don't think there were too many confident directors but you'd have thought that, just in case, there would have been a few bottles of champagne. If you don't use it you could give it to the players for putting up a great performance or whatever but your Kellys and your Whites obviously thought – no money back on the empties, so no champagne. Jimmy Steele saved the day, as usual.'

For every winner, there is a loser and McGrain's thoughts did eventually turn to the stricken Tynecastle team.

'It was about the Wednesday afterwards that I got round to thinking about them because the celebrations went on for days on end and we were busy accepting the plaudits, so I don't think I came down to earth for four or five days. It's a terrible thing to say but Hearts had their chance. I wouldn't say I didn't feel sorry for them because sorry isn't the right word. I'm sure Hearts wouldn't have felt sorry for Celtic if they had beaten us. Sorry is sympathy and I don't imagine Hearts would want my sympathy at all.

'But after the Scottish Cup final I appreciated the season they did have, going for the double and ending with nothing, which must have been very, very tough for their players. I wanted them to win the Scottish Cup against Aberdeen because we had taken the league championship away from them. That day I was a Hearts supporter and I felt sorry for them when they lost because they had put so much into that season and to be remembered for having won nothing was awful hard.

'Nothing I felt could change what had happened when all was said and done. We had won the league and it was an outstanding feeling. Certainly better than being a mechanical engineer. If I'd had five 'O'-levels maybe I would have never played for Celtic.

'And just imagine what would have happened if I'd only had one 'O'-level. I might have ended up a sports editor.'

Peter Grant

CELTIC I ATLETICO MADRID 2

2 October 1985

WHILE they waited for the players to appear before the start of a premier division match between Celtic and Aberdeen sometime around 1985, several of the press box crew were diverting themselves by trying to guess who would be booked first – Peter Grant or Neale Cooper – and when the yellow card might be administered. Three minutes after kick-off the pair were sprawled on the grass grappling with each other beside the goal at the Celtic end – Grant on top – but as the referee sprinted towards what looked like a Glasgow Saturday night punch up, the two snarling combatants smoothly transformed themselves into a pair of grinning choirboys just in time to assure the perplexed match official that what he had seen was a trick of the light which certainly did not require him to take up valuable space in his notebook.

They got off with a lecture about restraint although neither player was likely to let that shackle his instincts for long. They were a pair of remarkably similar personalities who could switch from Sunny Jim off the field to Mad Max on it. Grant, though, had the additional quality of endurance, a trait which enabled him to sustain a career at Celtic Park even when it was seriously threatened by hepatitis in 1988 or what at one stage looked like the probability of exile to England.

He maintains an active belief in God and has asked for assistance from that quarter when prospects looked unusually bleak but, by and large, the resources which have kept him at Celtic for more than a decade and fixed him in the affection of the supporters are to be found within his own robust physique and spirit. Grant is an uncompromising tackler, of challenges as well as opponents.

When Pat McGinlay arrived from Hibernian in July 1993 the new man was taken aback to be greeted by Grant with the words: 'Welcome to Celtic. I hope you like playing in the reserves.' McGinlay returned to Easter Road 18 months later having failed to displace Grant in the Celtic midfield.

Liam Brady, who wanted to sell Grant off to Norwich City, at a time when the player was on a month to month contract and weekly wages of £500, once showed him a team sheet which included his name and suggested that the best way to consolidate such an arrangement was to agree to the contractual terms he was being offered. Grant seized the sheet of paper, crumpled it and dropped it on the ground, saying: 'I'll still be here when you're gone.' The Irishman resigned as manager six months later.

Obviously this tenacity of purpose is liable to be viewed as admirable or aggravating without much scope for the middle ground but, according to Grant, Tommy Burns manages to combine both attitudes simultaneously. 'The gaffer and I have rows all the time. It doesn't worry me because I know that's exactly what he was like as a player as well – by the way, if he's going to be in this book, I hope he picks the game at Aberdeen where he got sent off and threw away his jersey.

'Seriously, I don't think it can bother him too much either because after we've had an argument I usually pick up a paper and read him saying that I'm doing well for the team. We might have regular differences of opinion but Tommy and Billy Stark are working night and day – that isn't an exaggeration – to get Celtic back to where it used to be. That's my dream and my ambition as well.'

Give me the boy until he is seven, runs the adage, and I will give you the man. Celtic were given Grant's allegiance from the day he was born, on 30 August 1965, and three months short of his seventh birthday the club helped to shape the future man's vision when they came within one kick of the ball of a third European Cup final under Jock Stein. That was the evening of 19 April 1972, when Celtic and Inter Milan found themselves stalemated after three and a half hours of goalless football and contested a penalty decider which went in the Italians' favour after Dixie Deans put his attempt high over the crossbar.

There was to be another Champions Cup semi-final two years later on the notorious occasion of the visit of Atletico Madrid, whose display of open thuggery – in particular the repeated assaults on Jimmy Johnstone – was a nauseating display. That was the last time Celtic came within reach of the highest European summit yet the memory of the vistas which had opened out amidst the peaks sustained many more extraordinary nights against Continental opposition at Parkhead, even when it became evident that there was no longer a team of Sherpas resident in the east end of Glasgow.

It is purely by coincidence that the game which has lodged most stubbornly in Peter Grant's memory also brought Atletico Madrid to Celtic Park, this time for a Cup Winners Cup-tie, but in almost every conceivable detail the contrast between the two games could not have been more marked. The most spectacular difference was that where 64,000 supporters had crowded into Celtic Park in April 1974, 11 years later the terracings and stand were deserted by order of UEFA.

Grant believes that the most bizarre European tie ever played at Celtic Park had profound consequences for the club. 'In my opinion, that game – and the three matches with Rapid Vienna which led to us being told we had to play behind closed doors – started the whole process which wore this club down and nearly made Celtic bankrupt.'

To perform in an empty ground was a particularly disconcerting process for a footballer who had dedicated himself to helping fill the place as a player and, who was in the beginning, an apprentice fan from Chapelhall, just outside Bellshill. 'Both grandparents ran Celtic supporters' buses so obviously the first step for me was to travel with them. I was in grey shorts at the time so I would have been about eight years old but it nearly came to an abrupt end because the first ever game I saw Celtic play was against St Johnstone at the old Muirton Park and we lost 2–1 (*this appears to have been a first division fixture at Perth on September 29, 1973*) and my grandfather said to me that I was never going to be taken back to see Celtic play again because I was obviously a jinx.

'Fortunately, he never held himself to his word so I was able to follow the team all over Scotland and it was the natural thing to want to play for the club – here I am now with 450-odd games for Celtic and it's been one of the greatest privileges I can imagine.

'Funnily enough, one ground I was never allowed to go to was Ibrox because my grandfather would say, "You're no' paying to get into that place because that would only give them more money to spend on players." So the first time I was ever at Ibrox was when I played there on my debut for Celtic in 1984. We boycotted Ibrox and that was just the way it was.

'I don't know where I would have ended up if Celtic had said to me that I wasn't good enough to make it with them, because they were the only team I ever cared about playing for, but I can't imagine I would ever have ended up with Rangers somehow, even after they started signing Catholic players . . . '

Grant's introduction to Ibrox was not auspicious because Celtic lost 1–0 but his zest for combative action coupled with an adaptability which has arguably been his greatest strength meant that he became a familiar component of the side the following season, when Celtic started another Cup Winners Cup campaign with a 3–1 aggregate victory over KAA Gent of Belgium. The draw for the second round inaugurated one of the most troubling passages of Celtic's European history when it paired them with Rapid Vienna.

For reasons which have never been obvious, meetings between Scottish and Austrian teams have intermittently generated undue aggression and sometimes blatant violence. Billy Steel was the first Scotland player to be sent off in an international match when he was dismissed a few minutes from the end of a 4–0 rout in the Prater Stadium in 1951 and 12 years later a match between the countries at Hampden had to be abandoned after brawling broke out on the field during what was supposedly a friendly fixture.

An undercurrent of confrontation marred Celtic's visit to Vienna on 24 October 1984. Frank McGarvey was the victim of a poisonous tackle by Kienast which left the Celtic forward writhing on the grass before he was taken off on a stretcher. Alan McInally was sent off in his first European game and three Celtic players were booked. The game ended in a 3–1 defeat but Brian McClair's goal offered Celtic reasonable hope of progress to the next round, which could be achieved with a 2–0 victory in Glasgow.

Rapid were equally alert to the percentages but they may have sensed a resolve in Celtic which made them wary. Their tactics were barren – slow play, possession football, reliance on the offside trap and time-wasting. Unpalatable as these devices may be, they have a history of goading Scottish teams into losing their patience, driven on by their exasperated fans. Celtic, though, looked like a side who knew that mastery of the contest was theirs.

With commendable maturity they probed the Rapid defence until McClair broke through on the half hour to reduce the aggregate deficit to 3–2. When Murdo MacLeod scored just before half-time Celtic were effectively ahead because of the away goals rule. After the break, with Celtic rampant, Rapid were cornered by their own cynicism, unable to lift themselves into a rhythm which might undo the damage they had sustained.

The Rapid goalkeeper, Ehn, spilled the ball and Tommy Burns scored the crucial third goal. The Austrians did not have the resources to retrieve the tie. More precisely, they did not have anything legitimate in reserve. At first their response was simply petulant and the villainous Kienast was sent off after a punch on Burns in the penalty area, although the Swedish referee did not award a penalty kick.

Rapid were clearly disintegrating and given the nature of the two games the referee's duty was to keep the proceedings moving as swiftly as possible towards their conclusion. His failure in this department was a poor advertisement for Swedish neutrality.

Ehn, the goalkeeper, tried to kick Burns. The referee decided to consult with his linesman but the pair were surrounded by swarms of players from both sides and so began the first act of a farce which would run for almost a year. It took a full quarter hour for the referee to come to a decision. During the interlude a bottle was lobbed on to the track from the Jungle.

Eventually a penalty kick was awarded which Grant, understandably in the circumstances, missed. Weinhofer, though, had spied an opportunity to exploit the disruption and after the match finally ended in an emphatic 3–0 victory for Celtic on the night and an aggregate 4–3 win which should have borne them into the next round, he materialised with a bandage on his head as a result – he claimed – of being struck by one of the bottles.

Video evidence showed that to be untrue but Rapid asked for Celtic to be thrown out of the tournament. UEFA's disciplinary committee ruled that Weinhofer had not been hit by a bottle but accepted that some had been thrown and fined Celtic £4,000. Rapid were fined £5,000 for their indiscipline and their coach, Otto Baric – a Yugoslav with a history of inflammatory behaviour – was banned from the touchline for the side's next three European ties. Keinast was suspended for Rapid's next four European ties.

And there it should and would have ended except that Rapid lodged an appeal, encouraged by by a tip-off that the committee's verdict had been a split decision. Capricious is one word for what happened next. At best UEFA's response was incompetent. At worst it was corrupt.

Only three of the 21 members of the appeal committee heard Rapid's case and Celtic's defence. This time the outcome was a stunner. The Austrians now declared that Weinhofer had not been hit by a bottle but by 'a small object'. It remained invisible on the TV replays and probably would not have been picked up by a microscope either. On the basis of this unsupported testimony the appeal committee came to the spectacularly ludicrous decision that the tie must be replayed at least a hundred miles from Celtic Park and that the fine on Rapid should be doubled.

Bad as this was, the most perplexing aspect of the whole affair to any Celtic supporter was the reaction of the board. Desmond White, the Celtic chairman, accepted the matter as a *fait accompli* and there were many who wondered why the directors were prepared to accept such a harsh injustice in a passive, not to say, abject fashion. Cynics held that the calculation was that since Celtic had already beaten Rapid comprehensively they would probably do so again, with the bonus of an extra gate from the huge crowd to be anticipated at Old Trafford, the venue for the third game between the sides.

At any rate, the game went ahead on 12 December with Celtic having to start again to overhaul the original 3–1 deficit from the first tie in Vienna. Their demeanour signalled that there was no chance of another overwhelming Scottish performance and although an Aitken shot ricocheted from the post after fifteen minutes Rapid got possession from the rebound, surged upfield and scored when Pacult rounded McGrain and Bonner. Celtic had never before lost both legs of a European tie and to make matters much worse two fans – both English-based – were able to climb over the perimeter fence and assault Rapid players. One of them was in the grip of two policemen who had secured his arms but not his feet, one of which he planted in a player's crotch as he left the park at full-time.

Celtic anticipated fearful retribution and a year later, in the aftermath of the Heysel disaster, they would almost certainly have had it visited upon them. Instead, UEFA chose to fine the club £17,000 and ordered that Celtic's next home game in Europe be played behind closed doors – effectively a supplementary fine of anything between £250,000 and £400,000. There was a certain amount of relief that a long ban had not been imposed but it was a bad end to a dirty business.

Rapid Vienna, meanwhile, went on to reach the Cup Winners Cup final and although there was undisguised pleasure at Parkhead when the Austrians lost 3–1 to Everton, it was accompanied by a hurtful sense that Celtic should have been the side to contest the trophy with the newly crowned English champions. The worst accusation which can be levelled against Rapid – one which still rankles with Grant – is that they cheated.

'That's the bottom line. It was one of the major disappointments I've had in my career. We went to Vienna and had Frank McGarvey carried off in five minutes. Alan McInally came on as a substitute for Frank and he was sent off. We could have been swamped in the first few minutes because they had Panenko who, as many people will remember, was a tremendous player and he kept us busy with free kicks from just outside the box. It seemed to me they hit the bar again and again at the start of the match because they threw everything at us but Brian McClair scored for us and despite all their good play we felt strongly we had a very good chance at home.

'You know what happened in the second game, especially me missing the penalty, but we were on form that night and I thought they had to start their tricks because they knew they couldn't cope with us. When Weinhofer appeared with the bandage on afterwards and said he had been hit with a bottle we knew that was a bit of experience on his part, making the most of anything which would give them an edge.

'We were worried about the bottle incident but the television replays showed that it had been at least ten feet away from him. We expected a fine for the bottle throwing but we weren't unhappy when we heard that Rapid had been fined more than us because that seemed fair. Then we had the appeal and the decision about the replay, which I couldn't understand because if they were held to be more guilty than us – which they had been in the first place – then why were we being punished by having a win taken off us and being made to start again at 3–1 down?

'I could even have understood UEFA saying that there was going to be a third tie and the winner on the night would go through, but we were in the position where everything we had achieved was taken away from us but they were back in the competition with an advantage. To be fair, when they got us at Old Trafford they tore us apart. There was no way back for us after that because they were leading 4-1 on aggregate, with an away goal, and even if we had somehow managed to beat them the result would never have been allowed to stand because of the two supporters who got on to the pitch and attacked a couple of their players.

'I've thought about this again and again and I really believe that the whole Rapid Vienna affair was the start of the disappointments for this club. We never really recovered from that for years. Europe is very special for this club – I know it's special for any club involved in the European competitions, but because of Celtic's contribution in the European Cup it matters more for us than maybe it does for a lot of other people – and we had our chance to play against the best taken away from us, not just for that season but the next year as well.

'It was the way it happened which mattered. Everything about the way it was done was a kick in the teeth for us and as I say, we never really came back from it. I suppose there are people who might think it's an exaggeration for me to talk the way I do about what Europe means at this club but put it this way – it's very, very hard for any team whose players are all the same nationality to win the European Cup. Will it ever happen for a team whose players are all Scottish? But Celtic did it and we remember that.

'I think that's something that will never be achieved again, even if Scottish teams win the European Cup on numerous occasions. So that was very special. The other thing about Europe is that it brings punters out to watch players they might never get another chance to see. I can think of world-class players I've come up against in Europe and anybody who's been watching Celtic in Europe for any length of time has seen many great, great players on that pitch out there.

'That's why when it was proposed to move this stadium to Cambuslang, I knew it would be a major disappointment for the likes of myself being brought up with Celtic, because all the wonderful memories are here. I'd have hated to bring my son along and say, "Well, we used to play down there – where the shopping centre is."

'I know 95 per cent of Celtic supporters feel the same way. I know we all feel it's so important to have stayed here. As far as European nights were concerned, they were particularly important to Celtic supporters who wouldn't always have taken their families to league games because there was always a wee bit of worry if the other side brought a big support with them, especially a bit further back when drink was allowed in and you would quite often get trouble between fans.

'But on a European night the support is almost always for the one club and it's a chance to introduce families to a very special atmosphere. There must be a lot of Celtic supporters who were first taken to the club to see European ties and they still think there's not a better attraction in football. That's the pull of the European league compared to what we have week in week out in our own competitions, to be quite honest. Don't get me wrong – I think we will always have to have our Scottish league and cup and so on but if we get the chance to have the very best players from other countries playing here on a regular basis we have to take it because everybody gets a buzz from that.

'For people who have been part of these magical nights we get at Celtic Park, the atmosphere is something they never lose. You've had Billy McNeill telling you that the stadium used to speak to you when it was empty. For me the feeling I got on big European nights started when I was a supporter coming to the ground down the London Road.

'That started when I was about 11 years of age, playing with the Boys Club up the London Road where you could see Celtic Park. When you're coming along that road – and I'm talking about a mile away – I would get that feeling in the stomach, the butterflies or whatever you want to call it, starting with the fellas who sell the scarves and flags, the lads wearing the green and white jerseys, some of them coming straight from work and eating their roll and chips.

'They don't have time to go home first or they don't want to because they're desperate for the game to start, they're all congregating at the same place every match, they all walk along the same route, they go into the same place in the ground. It's all the wee things which build up into what is waiting inside this ground, for them and for us.

'When I used to come here at first I was in the Rangers end because I wasn't allowed to go into the Jungle. Then when I got a wee bit older they let me into the Jungle and I would always meet the same people. You made your way up through the ranks when you grew up supporting the team and you had your own place where you stood. There might be 70,000 people here but you could always point to an exact point in the crowd and say, that's my place in the ground.

'To become a player and take part in nights like that – it's almost beyond words if you've been a supporter. You would get to the ground early and maybe walk out on to the pitch while it's empty and have a look at it. You'd take a deep, deep breath because you knew in a couple of hours it's going to be packed to the rafters and you knew where friends would be standing, probably in the same place you used to stand when you were one of the crowd.

'As far as I'm concerned, if you've been through all that everything here speaks to you about the importance of what you do for so many people who've been coming here for years. I still get that feeling when I pull on the jersey and when I run out there and look at it again. That's why we never wanted to move to some other ground. A major part of Celtic would have been lost if we had gone up the road to Cambuslang, I'm certain it couldn't have been the same for this club. That's why so many people were delighted when Fergus McCann came in and rebuilt the stadium.

'The best tribute you can pay to him is to say that when this ground is finished it will be the equal of the old Celtic Park. People who support other big clubs probably feel much the same about their own grounds but I think Celtic Park has an extra tinge of greatness because this was where we had the first British team to win the European Cup and, as I say, every one was a Scot, which makes us exceptional even among great clubs.

'Not that I don't enjoy going to other grounds where the atmosphere is special. Away from Celtic Park there's nothing better than going to Ibrox and hearing our fans in full voice, especially if theirs are so quiet. Having said that, I've had the experience which very few Celtic players will go through, of being at Ibrox when Rangers wouldn't let any of our fans in a couple of years ago.

'Only the chosen few of us know what that feels like and I hope nobody else has to. And we nearly kept them quiet. We did silence them for long enough but unfortunately for us they got a deflected goal late in the game to equalise late in the game. I remember the plane coming over with the big banner trailing behind it saying *Hail! Hail! The Celts Are Here!* and I got pelters from the Rangers fans that day because I pointed up to it and they went daft.

'I love that rivalry which is special to us, not in the bigoted sense of the word, but in the tension between the two teams which I hope never goes away. We have all these guys in Glasgow and throughout Scotland who are the best of pals at work during the week but if one supports Celtic and the other is a Rangers fan and an Old Firm game comes round, forget it. Friendship goes out the window.

'I really believe the whole Old Firm thing is getting better. The rivalry has changed in a good way. We don't get the crazy battles out in the street, although there will always be the few nutters who will do that, and I see more families at Parkhead and Ibrox so it looks as though we can still have a greater rivalry than almost anybody else but without the bigoted bitterness.

'I practise my faith and it means a great deal to me because I was brought up a practising Catholic. That's the way I want it to be and I feel as if it's helped me a lot. My faith has been a big part of my success, maybe the major part of it. There have been times when I have been really down, when you can only say so much to your wife or your friends – and perhaps you don't want to – and you need somebody else to talk to. For me it's the Lord and that's the relief it gives me. I go to chapel maybe three or four times a week. That's just me.

'Because I play with Celtic there are some people who say, "There's that Fenian bastard, Grant," or whatever. That's fine. If it gets up their noses that I go to chapel, OK. This club has always been known as a Catholic club because of our traditions and it probably always will be, but our most successful manager was a non-Catholic and two of our best ever players were non-Catholics, too.

'And I'm very, very proud to be a part of this club and to be able to say that. I'm also glad that the old bigotries seem to be softening but – and this is a big but – until Rangers sign a Catholic who goes to Mass two or three times a week, we're not going to know how much the strength of opinion has changed. I think everybody knows that Mo Johnston might have been a Catholic but if he went to chapel the place would probably fall down around his ears.

'Anyway, here I am wandering well away from the game we want to talk about – no' like me that, is it? – but what started me off was talking about Rapid Vienna being cheats, which is something that really goes against the grain for me and how they cheated our players and our supporters out of Europe not for one

135

season but for two. When we were drawn against Atletico Madrid
the year after we played Rapid Vienna we knew we were in for a
seriously hard couple of games.

'I'm not saying we would have beaten them if we had played in
front of our own support. I'm not saying we were a better team.
But we went to Madrid and we did very well over there so that
when we got back to Glasgow a goalless draw would have put us
into the next round. It's just impossible to be sure what would have
happened if we had played in front of a full house at Celtic Park
but we're entitled to wonder what we might have done. In the end,
the second leg against Atletico turned out to be the strangest game
I ever played in.

'We had actually played very well in the first leg in Spain. I was
still a young lad and for me to go to play against the likes of
Atletico Madrid – maybe they were in transition but they were
still a big, big club – was a dream. The setting in the Vicente
Calderon stadium was wonderful. It was way ahead of ours. We
came back here and I looked at the Jungle again. It used to have
that special atmosphere but it suddenly seemed small after
Madrid.

'When we were lining up to kick off over there I looked around
me and thought, this is what it's all about. It was like a huge bull
ring, the pitch was like a bowling green, the weather was warm
and I was desperate to get going because those are exactly the kind
of conditions you want to play in. Sure as fate, we went one down
but it was one of those games where you know you're going to get
back into it and I remember Davie Provan going down the line and
whipping a terrific cross into the box.

'There was Mo as usual with a great header and now it's 1–1.
They got a penalty kick, too, but as I said, we were in the sort of
mood which makes a team very difficult to beat and it seemed only
natural to me that Packie would save it, which he duly did. So we
came off at the end of the game with a tremendous result and we're
telling ourselves we're in with a right good shout when all of a
sudden it hit us that, hey, we're going back to play them in
Glasgow behind closed doors.

'We knew there were going to be major problems because on the
one hand there's nothing better than to have Celtic supporters
behind you, shouting you on in an important game and sometimes
intimidating the opposition players – and they can put the wind up
players who think they've seen it all before. But not to be able to

count on that, not to have the gee up you were used to get from the terracings, that was always going to work in Atletico's favour.

'It started long before we actually went on to the pitch. Even just going to the game was a weird experience. London Road was ghost-like. There were a lot of polis cordons because they had decided not to let any punters near the stadium and to be fair to the supporters, 98 per cent of them had heard that and decided not to go along so that nobody could say they had caused any problems. They had been warned that if they did turn up it could put Celtic into more trouble with UEFA, that the club could get fined or worse. It wasn't as though we could tell what might happen after the way they had handled the whole Rapid Vienna shambles.

'Also the game was an early afternoon match in midweek so people who were working wouldn't be able to get away without losing wages and it wasn't as though they were going to see anything. There wasn't much point in having the flu after lunch because the bosses would know what was going on. They all said to themselves, ach, we'll chuck it, we're no' going tae get in.

'So instead of the party atmosphere we were used to before a big European night, there was nothing. Nobody selling scarves or trying to tout people into a parking space, no singing, just nothing except polis. On the way to the game I started to get concerned. It worried me that this was going to be like a training session and that was exactly what we didn't want it to be. At the same time, the Atletico players must have thought it would do them very nicely.

'The worry was, how were we going to lift ourselves in an atmosphere like that? If I'm playing against the reserves, to give you an example, no matter how much we try to make it like a real game, I find myself pulling out of tackles because it's not the real thing. So we were all trying to convince ourselves that this was the real thing, a big European game which we could win if we just played the way we had done in the first leg, if we had that kind of confidence.

'I know people might ask why we had to do that. I mean, we are professional footballers so what difference did it make if there was a crowd or not? It was still a European tie and we were paid to be professional about it. My answer is that you do get used to routines before a game and there are things you notice but don't notice, if you know what I mean. The crowd noise is a good example.

'When you're in the dressing-room at Celtic Park you can hear it building up steadily before a game, but because that happens at every match you don't really pay much attention to it. You take it for granted. Before the Atletico game we were conscious of it all the time because it wasn't there, funnily enough. You could hear bits of conversations outside the dressing-rooms, or a door banging somewhere else in the building.

'We went out for the warm-up and when I looked about I saw guys who were in the first team some weeks – lads like Derek Whyte – standing about with ball boys' outfits on because we were not allowed anybody other than the players and officials. So Derek, who was still a young lad at that time, was diving over the walls and on to the terracings chasing after the ball.

'I was very friendly with Derek and when the game was under way I found myself going over to him to collect the ball for a throw in and thinking, this is very, very strange. In the game itself Atletico could play as though it was a training game because they knew it was getting to us. Of course, they had to score otherwise we were through on the away goals rule, at least, but you could see they were very relaxed whereas we were quite tense about it all.

'If there had been a crowd and you had made a mistake they would have been down on you, whereas we could only hear the manager. That itself was an odd one, being able to hear Davie Hay on the other side of the pitch. Normally you can hardly hear the guys nearest you, never mind somebody shouting from the dugout. And if there are 70,000 people on your back because you've played a bad pass, you're saying to yourself, God, I better no' do that again.

'Another thing which was offputting was the swearing. Players swear all the time during games but you can't hear it because of the noise. But if you did it in this game you could hear it reverberating all round the ground. That made it false, too. Talk about ghostly atmospheres – I've never experienced anything like it because although they let a hundred people in, they were almost all journalists and in those days the press were still up behind glass in the gantry so we couldn't hear them. At least in a training match you get people turning up, walking their dogs even, but there's still an audience.

'We were used to having our families there but we weren't allowed even that. I got one ticket, which actually I wasn't supposed to have, but I gave it to my sister Ellen, the only one who wasn't working or at school then, because she was a Celtic supporter who went to every game she could.

'We got a corner kick and I found myself wondering for a second why there was no roar. Normally you get that big surge from the fans which can lift you and maybe spark something off. But there was nothing apart from the shouts from our lads round the pitch, the ones pretending to be ball boys.

'We actually got off to quite a good start and nearly scored not long before half-time. Murdo hit the bar from almost underneath it (*from a Grant pass which Peter modestly chose not to mention*) He must have been about two yards out. Normally you would back Murdo to score from there ten times out of ten but the ball bobbled just as he was about to shoot and it came back off the bar and went over. Straight from the bye-kick they went up and scored.'

According to Ian Paul in the *Glasgow Herald*: 'From the beginning Celtic looke edgy and unsure of themselves, illustrated by their waving to an empty stadium before the kick-off. When Landaburo headed on to Bonner's bar in 13 minutes, the crowded press box, with Spanish commentators at times almost apopleptic, sensed that Scottish plans were not going to work out.

'There was a touch of fortune about the way Atletico's chance came about but not about its execution. Setien tried to slip the ball to Cabrera on the right but Burns stuck out a foot and blocked the ball, which bounced back to Setien who stepped forward and smashed a precise left foot shot into the corner of the net from 20 yards.'

For the second time in the two ties, Celtic had fallen behind. Grant was acutely aware that at their own ground Celtic had not discovered the self belief which underpinned their composure in Spain.

'We were saying to ourselves, we're out this time. With that goal everything was out the window. We had to lift ourselves and it was more difficult than I had thought it would be. It was almost impossible, to tell you the truth. We were up against foreign players who had the technique to knock the ball around all day if it suited them.

'The Celtic way didn't allow for that. Our crowd always wanted us to play as directly as possible but even with no fans here we just couldn't change our way. We were still doing cavalry charges and they had the sort of players who could just pick us off. There was quality throughout their team, although there were no outstanding big names. We got frustrated and Davie ended up making changes which he would never normally have done, to try and bring us back into the game.

'Of course, Atletico were also masters of time wasting and they did that as much as they could. One of their lads (*Quique*) was actually booked for it. Tom McAdam came on for Paul McStay and big Roy pushed up into midfield but they scored again almost right away and that was it. Finished. They scored it brilliantly, just went through us like a knife through butter.

'We did get a goal late in the game through Roy. Danny McGrain started it and gave it to Brian McClair, who cut it back for Roy to flick it into the net. It was all too little, too late. We needed to score three and there was never a chance we would do that once they were two ahead.

'So we were out of Europe at an early stage for the second year running. I'm not saying we would have won if we hadn't been playing behind closed doors. Maybe we would have lost anyway, but you have to say that the lack of a crowd was always going to be a big factor and in Madrid we had proved that we could play to their standard and get a good result against them in conditions which should have suited Atletico.

'It comes back to what I said about Rapid Vienna cheating. Rapid Vienna got to the final of the Cup Winners Cup the year before. Atletico Madrid got to the final the season we played them. Now we had beaten one of those sides on aggregate and drawn with the other on their own ground before we were forced to play in crazy circumstances. There has to be a chance that we could have gone on and done ourselves a right good turn in either season because there was nobody we feared. The way we played and with Mo and Brian up front we were usually value for a goal away from home in Europe, like we got in Madrid.

'That was a major blow for the team, being done out of the chance to see whether we could have handled it. And those two knockbacks were the start of bad times chipping away at this club because it took us a long, long time to recover from that.

'Since we're talking about Mo, I might as well say that another problem which took us years to come back from was him going to Rangers. We had been told he had come back from France to join us, we had paraded him to the press and everybody was pleased because he was a top-class striker, somebody Rangers hadn't been able to get – and they were signing just about everybody who moved at that time.

'I remember the last league game of the '88–'89 season was at St Mirren and we're going down to Love Street on the bus. Mo was on the coach to come and watch us playing and I said something or other to him about the next season and he said to me, "I've no' signed yet."

'I said to him, "You're joking." He said, "Naw, nothing's fixed." I couldn't believe it. I thought, aye, aye, there's somthing iffy going on here. Then I got called into the Scotland squad for the Rous Cup at the end of that season. We're at training and Mo said to me, "I'll be playing against you next season." I said, "What?" He said, "Aye, I'll be playing with Rangers."

'My first thought, because I'd been friendly with Mo the first time he was here, was, "Och, there's no chance of that." I thought it was a wind-up because Coisty was there, so I didn't take the bait. Next thing, he's on television walking into a press conference at Ibrox.

'That was a truly major blow for this club, a humiliation actually and very embarassing for us as players. We went six years after that without winning anything and I can't believe that would have happened if we'd had the likes of Mo up there to take chances for us. We were always renowned for having a proven goalscorer, the likes of Mo.

'What hurt me was that he had paraded himself in a Celtic jersey and told everybody how much he wanted to play in front of the Jungle. That hurt the fans and it hurt me because of how much I love this club. He had conned us and I hate when players say they're Celtic through and through and they don't mean it, because the first time they get an offer they're away.

'But hindsight is a funny business. Looking back now maybe it was a good thing because we eventually had to get back to basics. We lost Mo and then we got rid of too many experienced players, real Celtic men who might have carried the club. The backbone was gone. It came down to myself and Paul McStay and we found it very difficult because there were young boys and guys who knew nothing about Celtic coming in and looking up to us, whereas we had nobody to lean on out there. Our next port of call was the manager.

'Big Billy got the sack. Liam Brady comes in, doesn't know the traditions of Celtic Football Club. Then Liam goes. Joe takes over for a day. Joe goes. Wee Frank takes over for a week. Lou Macari comes in, yet again another strange decision at the time, because Lou hadn't played too many games for Celtic before he went to Manchester United.

'Then Lou went. And at last, with Tommy Burns and Billy Stark and Mr McCann, of course, we started from the beginning. Best of all we've become the fans' club again because after Mr McCann saved Celtic it was the supporters putting the money in which has let us rebuild the stadium and start buying the players we needed to compete.

'I've been through the hard times. I was there, same as I was there in an empty ground against Atletico. And one thing I can say with absolute certainty is that never again will we go through anything like that at this club. No more desperation. And no more empty grounds . . . '

Tommy Burns

CELTIC 2 DUNDEE UNITED 1

14 May 1988

TOMMY BURNS' MOST MEMORABLE GAME (Take One)

THERE was no problem in getting Tommy Burns to agree to talk about his most memorable game as a Celtic player. The real difficulty was to get him to actually do the talking. 'No bother,' he had said when the subject was first raised. 'I'll pick a good game for you.'

Weeks passed by and so did several reminders. The response began to vary. One day it would be, 'Right, we'll definitely do that.' A couple of days later Burns would say, 'What was it we were going to talk about?' Jo, his secretary, who has seen it many times before, tried to speed the process.

She telephoned one morning. 'He's got your letter on his desk,' she said. 'He'll definitely do it. He wants to do it.' Yes, but which game did he consider to be his most memorable? 'I'll get back to you,' said Jo. She did, in the afternoon. 'He says the problem is there are so many,' she said. 'But he will pick one out for you.'

Eventually a definite arrangement was arrived at. Tuesday morning, nine o'clock. On Monday afternoon Jo confirmed that the following day would not be a problem. What happened next morning was that, to adapt a line from Claude Rains in *Casablanca*, I was there at nine; he was there at 11.

'Come on in and we'll get on with it,' said Burns, oblivious to the two hour difference in our respective time zones. We sat down at his desk and from a holdall I produced the tape recorder and microphone plus one copy of Paul Lunney's invaluable *Celtic: A Complete Record* and one copy of the equally excellent *The Glory and the Dream* by Tom Campbell and Pat Woods. The books were backup in case he had not yet identified his chosen match but as it turned out, this was an unnecessary precaution.

'I think I would have to pick the Centenary Scottish Cup final as the game which meant most to me as a player,' said Burns.

An excellent choice – the Centenary Cup final, the game which completed a spectacular double and capped a hundred years of Celtic's existence with a victory forged out of adversity against Dundee United. A game remembered by everyone who was saw it and which must be even more deeply etched on the minds of those who played in it.

Or not.

To have seen at close quarters the transformation which has overtaken Celtic since March 1994 is to have witnessed time travel. In the two years after Fergus McCann bought a controlling share in the club, a few hours before it would have toppled into insolvency, a massive but moribund football institution was wrenched from the 19th century and hurled towards the 21st. A romantic but hopelessly outdated stadium has been demolished and progressively replaced by the mighty structure which now dominates the eastern skyline of Glasgow as impressively as the Clyde-built liners which once soared along the riverbank at the other end of the city.

And like a great Cunarder, the new Celtic enjoyed a spectacular launch when McCann floated the club and succeeded in achieving the most successful share issue in British football history with £26 million of fresh capital generated in a year. Sponsorship deals which were hawked off for buttons by the previous cash-starved board will command huge sums in future. The right to market Celtic replica strips is now valued at £15–£20 million. The season ticket base which had been almost dormant at a derisory 9,000 sales surged to 37,500 by the summer of 1996.

With McCann steering a high-speed course and Burns riding pillion there have been moments when a crash looked inevitable, especially when the two of them seemed to be wrestling for the controls immediately after the Scottish Cup final victory over Airdrie in May 1995. When they eventually settled into a working relationship which has been stimulating, if not always entirely comfortable, the club moved into a period of stability which had not been enjoyed for many years.

Under Burns Celtic went through the 1995–96 league season with the loss of only a single game, an extraordinary achievement. That one defeat was inflicted by Rangers, who also won crucial Old Firm encounters in the Coca Cola Cup and Scottish Cup, so although vast progress had clearly been made Celtic had to face up to the paradox that in terms of honours the season had actually been less successful than the previous year. For McCann it was a reminder that football may be a business but – to put it in business terms – market share is much less important than being the brand leader.

As if the pace of the revolution at Celtic Park were not enough to have to cope with, the European Court's ruling in the Bosman case meant that transfer deals would now involve long, complex and costly negotiations which could easily go off the rails – there was the salutary example of Jorge Cadete's protracted move from Sporting Lisbon.

Small wonder then that for most of his tenure as Celtic manager, Tommy Burns has appeared distracted. So many years of damage to undo and no extra allowance on the rule that there are only 24 hours in a day. So many demands on time and energy and too few calm moments. So many pressing reasons for the mind to drift off . . .

Which might explain why, ten minutes into discussing the Centenary Cup final, he said: 'I remember Billy McNeill had changed things around tactically and he'd put big Roy Aitken into the middle of the park to counteract Mark Walters. And we were underdogs – '

Halt right there! *Mark Walters*? *Underdogs*? Exactly which game are we talking about?

'When we beat Rangers 1–0. Joe Miller scored and –'

But Tommy, that final was in 1989. The Centenary Cup final was in 1988.

'Oh, aye . . . right. Dundee United. We won 2–1. Frank McAvennie got the goals. OK, start again. *That's* my most memorable game...'

TOMMY BURNS' MOST MEMORABLE GAME (Take Two)

Until Celtic win the championship there is every chance that interviews with Burns will include periods when he is present in body but not in mind. So for the benefit of any hapless outsider who does not want to have to use a Ouija board to make contact, the facts are these. Burns was born on 16 December 1956 in Calton, one of the oldest and toughest tenement districts in the heart of Glasgow. His football apprenticeship was spent with St Mary's Boys' Guild, Eastercraigs and Celtic Boys' Club and when he was 16 Celtic decided to send several of their promising youths off to the Junior ranks.

One or two went to Cumbernauld, another went to Ashfield, some to Linlithgow and Burns, like Danny McGrain and Paul Wilson before him, was despatched to Maryhill Juniors where he had a friend in Gerry Collins, who went on to become assistant manager at Partick Thistle and Falkirk. Burns' experience at Lochburn Park was considerably happier than Danny McGrain's, as recounted elsewhere in these pages.

'I had a smashing year there where we managed to win the league and we went far in the Scottish Cup and reached the final of the West of Scotland Trophy, so it was a great season for Maryhill who were basically a C Division team at that time. C Division was the bottom league and we managed to get ourselves into B Division.

'Basically I think the most important thing it did for me was to teach me to play against men every week. I came from under-16 football where you played against other boys like yourself and you could always hold your own. The challenge of junior football was that you were up against ex-pros, people in their mid to late twenties or early thirties and you had to learn how to handle yourself against players of that experience. So from that point of view I developed and became confident that I could develop and make an impact at a higher level.

'I wanted that higher level to be Celtic because as a boy I had been very much a supporter. I only lived about ten or 15 minutes walk along the Gallowgate at Soho Street where it was just natural to support Celtic as you grew up. I didn't see a great deal of games on a Saturday because I was usually playing but certainly any midweek games that I could get to, I was up here watching them.

'The first game I can remember was a Scottish Cup semi-final in the early Sixties. I can't remember the score or anything about the game but it was definitely away back then and I went along with a bunch of my pals. So it was in the blood to want to play for Celtic and I was very fortunate that most of the lads who went junior from the Boys' Club were called up together, which was great because we all came into the reserve team in a bunch.

'What was not so good was that at that time the reserve team was full of guys who were not able to get a game for the first team, which meant that the new boys were pushed further down the queue waiting for the chance to play a match, so the upshot was that I only made something like half a dozen appearances for the reserves that first year I was called up.

'At the end of the year seven of the lads who were called up beside me were released by the club, so I always thank God for the fact that in the last two months of that season I managed to get into the reserve team and played well in one game which was watched by Jock Stein. And then a mixed team of reserves and first team played against Clydebank and won 6–5. Davie Cooper played that night and scored three goals for Clydebank. Again I was in the team and played well and I think I just caught his eye in those last weeks, otherwise had I not been in those games and had he not happened to see them I think I would have been allowed to go like the rest of the lads.'

As a left-sided combative midfielder he would have been a considerable asset to any team but his passion for Celtic was both an advantage and a handicap. He made his first team debut as a substitute in a 2–1 defeat by Dundee at Celtic Park on 19 April 1975, but it took him two seasons to become a regular in the side and the temper which matched his fiery hair brought him into unacceptable conflict with opponents and authority so that eventually he reached a stage where he was ordered off three times inside 18 months.

'I don't think that I got wound up easily by opponents. I was always streetwise enough to know when that was happening but certainly I was on a very short fuse at that time and impatient – all the problems which you can feel as a young player when you're in a hurry to get where you want to go and you're trying to progress faster than your natural development will allow. In the early part of my career I had a lot of injuries which dragged me down a bit and it took me longer than it should have to become a regular with Celtic.

'I wasn't a regular until I was about 21 or 22, when I felt I should have been at 19 or 20, so there were a lot of frustrations there. Then you feel that when you do get in there you want to make an impression with the supporters and you tend to do daft things, but you find you get publicity for being controversial and you like that. And you think, oh well, this is what happened to George Best and people like him, so I'll have some of that.

'As you get older you start to realise what you want from your career and you know that you could end up as a guy who was here for a couple of years and then was away and was anonymous somewhere else. Or you could learn good habits, become a real professional, get to be a regular with Celtic, start winning things with Celtic and – the most difficult part of all – to become a Celtic player who's here for a long time. That takes a special type of person to remain here and play for this club over a long period.

'Some of that old feeling of impatience has come back to me since I've been a manager at this club. The supporters here have been starved of success for six or seven years. OK, we managed to give them a cup last year which whetted their appetite for more and this year I think we've made great progress in the quality of our play, but now I think I need impatience to drive me on and I don't see it as a bad thing at the stage this club is at. I want everybody here to be hungry and impatient but at the same time to channel it in the right direction.'

Before Burns' accession as manager the last time Celtic had succesfully harnessed such a deep-rooted zeal to outdistance Rangers and deliver a championship to the east end of Glasgow was in 1988. His recollection of that season (once he had cleared the 1989 Cup final from his mind) is of a momentum which seemed almost predestined.

'It was one of those years where it all seemed to fall into place steadily. There came a point where we started to look at what was happening and say to ourselves, this could be our year here. We got to the latter stages of the league and got into the habit of winning games late on. We got to the semi final of the Scottish Cup and won that very late on (*see Paul McStay's account of that game elsewhere in this book*) after losing a goal with about 15 minutes to go and then remarkably came back with two goals almost at the very end.

'And the same happened in the final against Dundee United. When games go like that they aren't only won on the day. Sometime earlier in the season we started to believe in ourselves and that we would make an impact in that particular year. It was one of those seasons where we had that very special bond with our supporters which seems to occur every so often.

148

'It happened in 1978–79 when Billy McNeill came back and in the last quarter of the season we'd had two or three players sent off in consecutive games, but even though we would go a goal down or a man down we would come back and win. You're right when you suggest that you have to be here as a supporter or a player or in the management to understand how deep it goes at this club. It's some sort of bond which is so strong that when it gets going you might as well try to stop a runaway train – that's how powerful it is.

'I believe these supporters are the best in the world and I mean that absolutely truthfully. But they're also very critical and they demand the best all of the time. You can't always give them the best but you can give of your best and the players who do best here respond to that. You want to be remembered as a player who was well thought of by these supporters. It certainly drove me on when I was a player, that I wanted to be regarded as a player who did well when things were against me as opposed to decorating a game when it was easy.

'I wanted to be seen as a player who could be relied upon by the supporters and by my team-mates in respect of going and getting the ball and trying to make something happen. It was about not being frightened to make mistakes or take criticism but giving everything you had. That's probably the definitive answer to questions about whether we play better in adversity because of our backgrounds. It was something that was bred into myself as a young supporter coming to this club and looking to what I might achieve and who I wanted to be.'

Celtic's 1988 league and championship double assumed such a momentum that by the final weeks of the season there was a powerful feeling of predestination about their progress, but even destiny requires to be coaxed on its way. In retrospect – and with a manager's perspective – Burns now regards Billy McNeill's handling of the side on the run-in as crucial.

'He used the players at the right times, he didn't overplay us. He changed it about tactically at the right time and got a nice bit of freshness into the squad. In the Scottish Cup run we actually had a much tougher start than most people usually remember because we began with Stranraer here and that was supposed to be a walkover for us, only Stranraer didn't want to be walked over and we scraped through 1–0 with a Frank McAvennie goal.

'Then we got another home draw and this time it was Hibs and again we didn't do so well. Maybe we were a wee bit tense in front of our own crowd but that game finished 0–0 and so we had to go to Easter Road for the replay, a very difficult game which we won 1–0. Peter Grant had the strike at goal and he claims he scored and Billy Stark only got his head to it when it was in. I was claiming the goal because I squared it to Grantie.

'And it went on from there. We beat Partick Thistle 3–0 at Firhill. I scored and so did Billy Stark but Peter Grant couldn't claim anything in that game because Andy Walker got the other goal. It was Hearts next, we've spoken about that and so we went on to the final against Dundee United. The press build-up was very predictable. On the one hand it was all about us getting a double to celebrate our hundredth birthday and on the other it was about how Dundee United kept getting to finals and losing them.

'We read about how United were going to change their routine to see if that would do the trick, that Jim McLean wasn't going to travel with them to the game, that they were going to travel down a different route and stay in a different hotel. The one thing which stayed in my mind throughout all the hype before the final was that here was me, 31 years old, maybe never going to get another opportunity to play in a double-winning team.

'I thought about that all the time in the lead-up to the game, even during the game and most importantly after it, when I felt a real sense of achievement.

'Dundee United might have been worried about their build-up but we just went through our usual routine. We stayed at Seamill, had a wee game on the front lawn and the lads who lost were into the water. That was the penalty for losing but I was never one of those guys. I always enjoyed a good roar at the ones who were being thrown in.

'We'd been to a good few Cup finals during the Eighties. That was our fourth and we had got into a kind of tradition about how we approached them. But as I say, what I couldn't get out of my mind was that I wanted so much to be a part of a double-winning team because that's something which is truly memorable and it would be a statement which could be made by this team – and a very, very good team it was.

'Something which worked quite well for me was my age and experience. I had got to the point where it was time for me then to enjoy the Cup final. I made a decision to make the most of it and I thoroughly enjoyed all of it, from the feeling of getting up on the morning of the game when the press were there and all the TV cameras were around.

'We had them on the bus and following us into the ground, building up the atmosphere for the people who were watching and listening. I honestly think I savoured every moment of it. If it had been earlier in my career, when I would find myself suddenly in a Cup final with Celtic, the occasion would have been more tense for me. In those days, your thoughts were more likely to be that you must win the game for this club and above all, you mustn't lose it because it's so, so important.

'You learn that they're all important anyway but I think always that you play better when you're more relaxed. You have to tell yourself that this is an opportunity most players never have a chance to enjoy so you've really got a duty to yourself to make the most of it, whereas when you get too tense you go and worry about it. That's when you discover, maybe too late to do anything about it, that it's very, very easy for the whole thing to pass you by.

'I had a pretty set routine before I would go out on to the pitch but I never got to the stage, which some players do, where I would think, "Oh no, I'm not going to play well today because I didn't manage to get my strapping on until 23 minutes past two." Basically, I had a rough routine but it could vary over the seasons. I liked to relax myself by putting the oil on or getting somebody to give me a wee rub down.

'I think at that stage of my career I was into sitting in the bath for ten minutes before the game. That was to let the warm water do its work and get the blood flowing through the legs before I would give them a nice gentle stretch. After that it was a case of, right, that's me ready, now I'm going to go out there and enjoy this game.

'A Scottish Cup final always has a very special atmosphere for players, anyway. You've played your whole season, you've done all your hard work and got to wherever you've finished in the league. If you were in the position of Celtic in 1988 then you've won the championship and this is a great bonus, but I'm sure Dundee United felt much the same as we did. There are no more games to come, the season is finished after this match, it's been the only game anybody's been talking about for the last week or two and you've had nothing to do but get yourself in the right frame of mind for it.

'Then the whistle goes and there's no more talking or hype and you're getting on with it, doing your job, trying to get a good touch of the ball early on, maybe put in a strong tackle or get the ball away to the forwards to let them give your supporters a chance to build up a roar right away. Before you know it you've settled into the game and if you're experienced you just let that happen to you.

'The pattern of the game was pretty even. I felt we had the upper hand in the first half as far as possession goes and it seemed to me we were playing the calmer football. I thought at that stage that United were really trying to stop us playing to some extent and they were harassing us a lot. At that time it was in my mind to get myself on to the ball as much as possible because I wanted us to start making passes just to try and coax us into a rhythm and give us some cohesion.

'There wasn't much happening around the goals but at half-time I was quite happy with the way we were performing. It was going well and we were in the ascendancy so we weren't looking to change anything too much after we went back out. And again, I thought we started pretty well but when we didn't score the game went into a bit of a lull.

'I remember United setting up an attack but not being too bothered about it because we had been dealing with them fairly easily, but in this case there was a clearance which Eamonn Bannon headed back in right towards our goal. And to my surprise Kevin Gallacher managed to get a yard on Roy Aitken and he pushed on to fire an unsaveable shot into the net.

'The problem for Roy had been that he couldn't touch Kevin. Roy had been booked earlier in the game so if he got another card he was off, which was what had happened to him two or three years earlier against Aberdeen (*see also Aitken's account of the 1985 final*), but as I say, at the time I was amazed at the fact that he managed to get away from Roy.

'I think Roy was actually on the turn as Kevin was running on to the ball so maybe that was the reason. I remember Roy chasing him. I thought, you won't get away from Roy, that's a certainty. But just as Roy reached him Kevin hit the shot. Again, what made it awkward was that he hit the ball with his left foot while he was going through the inside right position, so in the end it was a smashing goal.

'I certainly wasn't expecting it and what happened then was that the feeling overcame me that we really had to go for it now. I told myself I had to get on to the ball and make something happen. And that took me out of the lull, whereas before I had just been playing in the game, moving along and passing it like everybody else. The goal put it in my head that I had to take responsibility, pick it up and run the risk of losing the ball.

'By that stage of my playing I knew that you have to decide to take that risk because if you do lose the ball it's happening for the right reason, that you're trying to change the game and trying to create something. And the fans know it, too. They sense it and they encourage you to go ahead and do it. So the roar went up from our fans and really, from that point we just got better and better.

'I was conscious of our crowd in that game, as I was quite often at Hampden, because you know that it's from that the expectancy comes. You're going towards that goal down at their end and you're pushing yourself to get the extra weight in a tackle, or the extra surge that means you can get a cross in or be individual and create something dangerous.

'Once we got going after Dundee United's goal it was simply wave after wave of attacks. The game got into the same kind of pattern as the 1985 final, as Big Roy has described to you. United had got their goal and they probably weren't going to get another one, although we always had to be aware of the danger of them breaking away because that was their trademark, so we felt that if we got one goal we should be able to go on and win because the crowd were willing us to do it.

'Plus, we had come from behind so often that season, in important league games and especially in the Cup semi-final which was a few weeks before that game, that we knew – we really just knew – that we were going to get that winning goal sooner or later.'

Again, Billy McNeill had seen that although the fates still favoured Celtic after they fell behind, reinforcements would not go amiss. On came Billy Stark and Mark McGhee to replace Derek Whyte and Andy Walker with 20 minutes left to play. Within five minutes the contest swung towards Celtic. With United steadily retreating into defensive layers across their own half Anton Rogan found room to push along the left across the halfway line. United paid a heavy cost for allowing him so much room. Rogan crossed, McAvennie leapt and swept a fine header away from Billy Thomson in the United goal. As he saluted Macca's equaliser Burns felt something go out of United's spirit.

'Yeah, it was quite a definite sense that they had lost it and to be fair, it's very, very difficult for any other team to come to

Glasgow and take on the Old Firm. When you've got that mass of supporters behind you, with all the passion they show, it's something which permeates the whole day and then the whole of the ground. As soon as you kick off you know you have that energy working for you. You've got to go with the flow.

'And it's tremendously hard for other clubs to cope with that, especially if they lose anything because then the whole atmosphere shifts up another 20 per cent, your crowd's flying and the noise is unbelievable. I couldn't be definite and say that was the loudest I've heard the Celtic fans at a final, because there have been a few occasions when they've created bedlam, but it certainly was an incredible noise.

'It was very hard for United after that. Maybe not impossible, but not too far off it. They started looking for leaders then and more and more they were going into a shell and we could see that. It was obvious from within their framework and the way they started to play. They were just kicking the ball on and hoping they would get something out of it and that was when we knew we had the bit between our teeth and that if we didn't let go we would win it.

'I knew time was going on and that the game was nearly finished but I always thought we would get another goal. It comes back to this habit we had got into that if there were 30 seconds left on the clock, we would use them to go up and score.

'And we did it again. Last attack of the game, we're buzzing around their box, they're desperate to hold on till the final whistle and they're very, very tired but we're not feeling any signs of fatigue at all, because we know we're going to get that goal. Frank McAvennie gets the ball, sees a wee gap in their defence, shoots – and that was it, 2–1. We've won the Scottish Cup with the last kick of a hundred years. What a way to finish that was. But that's absolutely typical Celtic.

'The final whistle blew more or less immediately and my thoughts were to go straight to the Celtic support. Grantie and I had a wee dance round about the Celtic end and I can remember Big Roy having to shout at us because it was time for the team to go up and get the Cup and be given our medals. It was a feeling of pure happiness because we had won a double and deep down I knew the chance probably would never come again for me to be part of that.

'From that point of view I felt that by the age of 31 I was entitled to a great sense of achievement. When people look back to the history of this club and see the Celtic double-winning team of the centenary year, Tommy Burns will be in it.'

If this book has a motto, it is probably – 'Cometh the hour of victory, cometh Jimmy Steele with the bubbly.' Time and again the Celtic masseur took it upon himself to make sure that if his boys won a trophy, they should be able to celebrate in traditional fashion. The 1988 final was no different and Burns reflected that some aspects of life at Celtic changed little over a hundred years.

'Aye, Steelie was always the guy who had the champagne and that day was not any different. It became a bit of a tradition and the old board were fully in favour of Steelie paying for the champagne. Mind you, it wouldn't have mattered if he had forgotten that day because we were all drunk with happiness. That night we went to Mark McGhee's house because Mark had a party there. I never drank that night.

'I didn't take a drink. I maybe had a drop of shandy at the beginning but after that I just took Coke because I was so happy and I wanted to enjoy the moment and I didn't want anything to take away that feeling. It was a feeling that lasted me for days on end.'

Euphoria was epidemic amongst Celtic supporters and also in the boardroom. The directors had been seriously alarmed by the revival of Rangers under Graeme Souness, who had steered them to the championship and League Cup in his first season as manager at Ibrox in 1986–87. Rangers retained the League Cup, the first honour of the 1987–88 season, but they could not sustain their momentum and Celtic's triumphant double was a magnificent end to a remarkable century.

Billy McNeill was quoted in the *Celtic View* as telling his players: 'Have a good holiday, unwind a little and get the events of the last ten months out of your system. We have set ourselves standards and those standards must be maintained.'

The directors could not have agreed more fulsomely or more gratefully. Yet, it was at this heady moment for Celtic that the seeds of misery were sown. The only significant addition to the playing staff that summer was Ian Andrews, who was brought from Leicester City as cover for Packie Bonner after the Irish goalkeeper sustained a back injury.

The reversal of fortune which followed was as numbing as it was complete. The new season had hardly begun when on 25 August Rangers inflicted a traumatic 5–1 hammering in the Old Firm derby at Ibrox. As the goals rained past the unfortunate Andrews, Burns turned to the power of prayer.

'It was,' he said afterwards, 'as awful an experience as I have ever had against Rangers. In the second half I just prayed and prayed that they wouldn't get seven.' God may move in mysterious ways but that afternoon the saving grace for Celtic was that Rangers fielded six Englishmen and none of them understood why – when they had already scored five – their fans were screaming at them to make it eight.

The imports had heard nothing about the 1957 League Cup final. To use more familiar words, they did not know the history. However, they had signposted the future and at this distance Tommy Burns believes that Celtic underestimated the resources which would be needed to keep pace with Rangers, never mind overhaul them.

'I think there's never a better time to invest than when you're doing well because when things are going badly it becomes a big risk and also it can be looked on as a panic measure. So you're always better to strengthen when you're on the ascendant.

'And I well remember at that time speaking to Tommy Craig and Tam saying he was hopeful that we could have gone and got Peter Beardsley and Paul Gascoigne, funnily enough. I don't need to say any more than that. Had we got Beardsley and Gascoigne in '88 God knows what Celtic would have gone on to achieve. It might have cost them a great deal of money by the standards of those days but it would have been money well, well invested.

'But we all know what happened. After I left Celtic in 1989 and when the really bad days set in here, I was very disappointed to see a club of this stature so enveloped in apathy, which ultimately was what happened here. I watched it as a Kilmarnock player and obviously the standards had dropped but it became quite alarming, to the point where Celtic came to Kilmarnock and we beat them 2–0 with a very ordinary team but one which worked hard.

'It got to the stage where Celtic players weren't motivated at all, for a variety of reasons – and there were a lot of reasons – but that was the biggest disappointment for me, that a great club had slumped to its knees and there didn't seem to be any way out for them. Possibly the biggest indictment was that there was no passion within the team.

'I knew there were people like me here. Paul McStay, Peter Grant and Packie Bonner were here and nobody can fault them for what happened but it's very difficult for three players to lift eight or nine. It's much easier for eight or nine to bring three down to their level and in a lot of cases that's what happened. I did think long and hard about what I would have done if I had still been there.

'Even as a player I would have had a war every day in there because of the fact that this club was being laughed at and becoming non-effective and with no credibility. Basically, Celtic became just another club, no different from any others in the premier division. The only difference might be that we still had our supporters.

'When the call eventually came from Celtic I did feel that it was part of the purpose of my life, funnily enough. I think that God has got our way planned for us probably since the beginning of time. I don't know why God has chosen me to come here and be involved but they say that when He wants to do something in the eyes of man He chooses a worthless thing and makes great things happen through that. Maybe He couldn't have chosen anything more worthless than me, eh?'

How, though, the question might reasonably be asked, does Tommy Burns square his sense of the accomplishment of the work of God at Celtic with the daily lies and deceits which are and always have been part of the managerial process?

'Well, I don't think I have to tell many lies here. If the press come and say that they've heard I'm trying to sign a certain player and I don't want that knowledge made public then, aye, I would tell a lie because if that falls through then I'm the one who ends up with egg on my face and Celtic may have been made to look daft.

'I don't really feel that's lying. It's part of the football syndrome, if you like, and anyway I don't need to lie to players about anything. I tell them what I feel and if they don't like it, so be it. At least they know what I honestly think and I always think that relationships with people are better when they realise they can come to you and say what they think and you will keep it to yourself.

'I do feel strongly about how Celtic and Rangers conduct themselves. Unfortunately, there will always be people who bring their children up to hate Celtic or to hate Rangers for no other reason than the fact that we're Celtic and they're Rangers. I think you've got to be a bit more open-minded than that and realise that we're both football clubs and that there should be no reason to hate another club purely because their supporters to a different church or whatever. As far as I'm concerned God's the same for us all and He'll judge the whole lot of us.

'It's good to have a rivalry and there is none greater for this club than against Rangers and vice versa for them. But equally I don't see why if they're doing good things we can't put our hands up and say, hey, they got their act together, put down a firm foundation, got a sound leader for their club – somebody who likes to be one up on us, which is understandable because we'd certainly like to be one up on them – and give credit where it is due.

'We've got our club which we think is special, with different traditions and a different mentality from Rangers but I would always stress to our supporters to love Celtic and bring their children up to do so because ultimately we believe we stand for good things in football. I hate the vindictiveness, the vitriol and the evil that the decent people on both sides – which is most of the supporters – have had to put up with on certain occasions.

'What I will also say, though, is that in all the years I have lived here in Glasgow very, very rarely have I ever had hassle from Rangers supporters. Sure, they want to wind you up, talk about your team, their team, whatever. It's different when supporters get to an Old Firm game. Then a lot of old feelings and passions come out, but I've never thought they spend all their time thinking about it from week to week.

'It's the wolf pack mentality. One or two on their own are no problem but once they get together in numbers they go absolutely mad. We'll never change that. But there are good things going on in both clubs. Walter Smith at Rangers projects the right image for somebody who's in charge of a big, big football club – humble, forthright, economical with words but says what he thinks and is capable of looking at both sides of an issue and giving credit where it's due.

'And I hope that I'll be able to do the same job at Celtic Football Club. I think about it every day and I will do so until this club has been restored to the position it deserves to occupy.'

Tommy Burns did not survive two consecutive seasons without a trophy success. He lost his job as Celtic manager in May 1997. Three weeks later he joined Newcastle United as youth coach under his former teammate, Kenny Dalglish.

Paul McStay

CELTIC 2 HEART OF MIDLOTHIAN 1

11 April 1988

IF the past is a foreign country then Paul McStay was born and brought up on its frontier. It could not have been any other way for him or his brothers, Willie and Raymond, in a family whose name had been illustrious in Celtic's chronicles for half a century since their great-uncles became a byword for loyalty and enduring service to the club.

When the original Willie McStay was signed in 1912 he came from Larkhall Thistle and the family maintains its connections with the Lanarkshire town to this day. Some might view this as a triumph of tenacity over experience in an area where the Orange Order could never be confused with an instruction to deliver fruit, or where sashes were only what kept the windows in place.

As Andy Cameron put it when the comedian presented Paul McStay with his award as Scottish Football Writers' player of the year in 1988, 'He's going to use the money to build the Larkhall Bypass . . .'

As it happened, back in the early years of the century Celtic almost bypassed the original Willie McStay even after they promoted him from the Junior ranks. Rangers won the league in his first season at Parkhead but Celtic took the title the following year and went on to win another three consecutive championships during the First World War. Willie could not break into the side at first and he was loaned to Ayr United (with an interlude at Belfast Celtic) until 1916 when his maturing talent combined with the inevitable shortage of footballers during the hostilities caused Celtic to recall him.

He was a forceful player, strong and versatile in defence. When the tank was introduced as a war weapon the Celtic supporters immediately borrowed its name to describe their most robust tackler. It was Willie McStay who laid the deep foundations of the family connection with Celtic by making almost 500 appearances for the club. By the time he was transferred to Hearts at the start of the 1929–30 season he had won four championship medals and three in the Scottish Cup. Those were the prizes which would be touched and treasured by his great-nephews 50 years later.

Jimmy McStay, Willie's younger sibling, followed him to Celtic Park by the same route through Netherburn Juniors and Larkhall Thistle. Like his older brother he was not exactly an instant success. He played nine games in the autumn and early winter of 1922 but when Celtic were badly beaten 3–0 on 30 December he was one of the scapegoats and was dropped from left half. In fact, Jimmy was well out of the following three fixtures because they ended in defeats by Rangers (0–2), Aberdeen (1–2) and Third Lanark (0–1).

It was clear that wherever the problem lay it could not be blamed on one man and Willie Maley, the Celtic manager, persuaded his sceptical directors that he should persist with Jimmy. After some trial and error to find his best position, which included spells at right back and right half, Jimmy was settled at centre half although he was employed at full back when the need arose and he went on to come close to equalling Willie's appearance total with over 450 games for the club. By the end of his career he had one championship medal and five more from successful Scottish Cup campaigns.

Celtic supporters grew familiar with the sight of the pair playing alongside each other in defence and their service to the team included the captaincy, Jimmy succeeding to the skipper's role in 1929. Both men became managers, Willie with Glentoran in Northern Ireland and Jimmy with Celtic during World War II.

For the next generation of McStay brothers to play together for the club bedtime stories would consist of tales of the exploits of their great-uncles. They form Paul McStay's earliest memories.

'It was when I was very young, maybe even before I started school, in fact, that my dad used to tell us about our connection with the club, about our great-uncles and about Celtic itself. Then we started to go to games and I think by that point we were caught up in the passion of the place. We didn't have too many pictures of my great-uncles – pictures were a bit scarce – but I did get to hold a couple of medals which, when you're a young boy, is such a thrill. I remember when I had just started school that I was already writing *Celtic!* on my jotters, so when people say that this club is in our blood I don't think it can be denied.'

The old argument about whether nurture is more important than nature cannot be resolved by studying his childhood. Football claimed him both ways and by the age of seven McStay was established as the youngest member of the team at St Mary's primary school in Larkhall.

'We won the Charity Cup when we beat another local school, Glengowan Primary. I was eight and Willie was 11 so he was one of the veterans. It was the first time the school had won the trophy in 33 years, I think, and that was my first success. That's the earliest memory I have of actually playing football so I knew what it was like to win a trophy at an early age.'

By the time he reached Holy Cross secondary school in Hamilton and combined his football there with appearances for Hamilton Thistle amateurs the word was out amongst scouts that the McStay dynasty was flowering again. Several senior clubs indicated their interest in enticing him away from the family tradition but his allegiance was as indelible as a tattoo and he was destined for Celtic Boys' Club.

'Actually, I first came in here full-time on a job creation scheme. I wasn't supposed to leave school until Christmas that year but my teachers helped me to get away early because although the scheme was only supposed to bring me in here one or two days a week from the start of the season I ended up latterly being in every day. To be honest, the teachers seemed to recognise that there wasn't much chance of me doing well in exams but they saw that I had an opportunity to succeed here, so I've always been grateful to them for letting me get on with it and to Billy McNeill for encouraging me at the same time.

'A lot of the lads my age in the Boys' Club were Celtic supporters of course but most of them didn't get to see the team in action too much because they were playing at the same time as there were games on at Celtic Park. For me, though, it was one of the most enjoyable ways I could spend time, coming to see games here. For long periods before I actually joined the club I wouldn't play on a Saturday afternoon although I had opportunities to be in the under-14 and under-15 teams at that period. I would much rather play for the school in the morning, jump in the supporters' bus, watch Celtic in the afternoon and play for Hamilton Thistle on the Sunday. For me that was the perfect weekend.

'Actually, the first game I remember seeing wasn't a good one for Celtic. It was the League Cup final in 1975 when Dundee beat us and Gordon Wallace scored the only goal of the game. I was in the North Stand at Hampden that day. It was pouring with rain and freezing cold, a bad day all round. I think the reason that match has stuck in my memory is because at that time we were used to Celtic winning so much.

'When I came here with my dad we used to stand – well, I used to sit on a barrier when I was wee – at the corner of the Rangers end next to the Jungle and when I started to go on my own or with a couple of pals it was to number eight in the Jungle, which by coincidence turned out to be the number I ended up wearing for the team for many years.

'The first time I ever saw an Old Firm game I actually came in through the front door here. I had an injury and I had to come in and let Brian Scott have a look at it. It turned out there was an Old Firm match so I was delighted to get to see that. Then my dad let me start going to see the Old Firm play when I was about 15. I went to Ibrox a couple of times but it was a restriction my parents put on me, that they weren't too keen on the idea of me being at those matches because there was sometimes a bit of trouble.

'My first time at Ibrox was a 2–2 draw. I was standing in the enclosure and we were even louder than we would have been at Celtic Park because we knew the team was in enemy territory and they would need all the backing we could give them.

'I came to a few here when you could still get lifted over at the gate and we did the usual thing of standing on beer cans to get a better view. The best one of all was when Celtic beat Rangers 4–2 to win the league in their last game of 1979. I was up the Celtic end. What a night that was, completely emotional. Then I raced home to watch the highlights.

'What happened there? They were never shown, supposedly because of a television dispute, but I've got a few suspicions about that one. It was a wee bit of a damper on the night. There must have been a few Rangers fans pulling the wires out at STV or something, just to spoil it for us.

'I'm like every other supporter. Even before I became a player I thought that European nights were extra special and the one which was most memorable for me was when Celtic played Real

Madrid (*5 March 1980, a 2–0 victory for Celtic; Real Madrid won the second leg 3–0*) I got to the Jungle early that night just so I could savour the atmosphere properly, especially because we were up against such a famous club.

'That was a fabulous night for every Celtic supporter and it was very unfortunate the way it eventually worked out. Even so, that gave me a real taste for the European games and it didn't change when I was playing in them. Every club wants to be involved in Europe but because of what happened here in the European Cup in 1967 I would say they do have an extra edge at Celtic Park. You really never stop getting excited about European ties.'

McStay could hardly have failed to be enraptured by his own debut appearance on that stage, against a club whose name is as resonant as that of Real Madrid. In the first round of the 1982–83 European Cup Celtic met Ajax Amsterdam, drawing 2–2 at Celtic Park and winning 2–1 in Holland (*the game chosen by Packie Bonner for this book*).

Although there was an interruption of the sequence by the advent of the so-called New Firm of Aberdeen and Dundee United, for the 22 years after Jock Stein's first league success in 1966 Celtic fans had seen their side qualify for the European Cup two years out of three, an extraordinary rate. The appointment of Graeme Souness at Ibrox in 1986 threatened that pattern, especially when Rangers won the title the following season, so Celtic's dramatic response in the spring of 1988 was of exceptional importance to their supporters.

By 11 April the Centenary double was within touching distance. A 2–0 home win against St Mirren six days previously meant that another premier division victory would almost certainly see Celtic take the title back from Ibrox. A quirk of the fixture list meant that back to back fixtures against Hearts – in the Scottish Cup semifinal at Hampden Park, then in the league at Tynecastle, would have a crucial bearing on Celtic's prospects. Like Tommy Burns, McStay (who by that time was playing at such a consistently impressive level that he would soon be voted player of the year by his fellow professionals as well as the sports writers) emphasises the role of Billy McNeill in reviving the team and steering it through a shoal of tough contests.

'I had always seemed to get on particularly well with big Billy and I definitely responded to him better than to almost anybody else. I was disappointed to see Davie Hay going the summer before but football can be cruel and Billy coming back gave the place the lift it needed for our centenary year. It really was a lively environment because the front area of the ground was upgraded and modernised and on the pitch Billy and Tommy Craig worked us very hard.

'I had been coming towards the end of my contract when Billy came back and I wasn't sure how my future was going to work out. I wanted to stay with Celtic more than anything but I also wanted to be sure the club was going to move in the right direction. When he returned from England I had no doubts. I think it's quite well known that I offered to renew my contract for another ten years and Billy suggested it might be wiser all round to keep it to five years, but that shows how positive I felt about the club that year and how good the atmosphere was here.

'Billy and Tommy brought new players in, which made the rest of us feel that something fresh was happening, and we put in a particularly hard pre-season. That's what sticks in my mind about the way we approached the centenary year. We really put a great deal into working at our system, closing opponents down and playing properly as a team when we went away to Sweden to prepare. We reaped the benefits of that later in the season.

'We came back from the Swedish trip and we were thumped by Arsenal in a friendly which was a bit worrying for some people who couldn't really see what we were up to, but when the season got under way we started well at Cappielow with a 4–0 win in our first league game and we picked up steam from there. There was a good professionalism about every player in the team at that time and a determination, which was just as important.

'I felt there was a togetherness about the squad which made a difference over the season. We had our tussles in training and the usual wee disagreements like any other team but nobody took the huff about an argument. We all got on with our jobs which is what I mean by professionalism. It was because of the good relationships within the squad that you could speak your mind freely.

'People said what they thought and nobody took offence, which is the way it should be. I can look back and say honestly that we had no problems to speak of inside the squad. More than anything, I would say that was why we did so well that season, because we had a real spirit which pulled us through in games where we might not have won otherwise. The spirit was brilliant.

'We did simple things away from the football to nurture that feeling. We had a couple of golfing days and meals out to help cement the togetherness we all felt but for me more than anything it's about how players get on when they're training and working together. We spent a lot of time doing physical rotuines and shadow work and everybody was tuned in to that as well. For those sort of things to be successful you must have players with the right attitude, players who want to achieve.

'Charlie Nicholas says that when he came into the team there was a similar feeling, the lads mixed well on and off the park and they could be relied on to play for each other. I came in just after Charlie, two or three years or so, and I felt it, too. There was an eagerness and a hunger about the place, the same feeling we had in '88. And then, of course, we also knew what a special year it was going to be for the club, so that was another motive to do well.

'Once you get that confidence you get into the way of doing your work correctly and well. It actually got hard for us to lose games in '88. Even if we were a goal down with five minutes to go people were still looking for a win. In the game we're going to talk about my dad was in the stand and he turned to the guy next to him when we were losing with three minutes left to play. He said to this man, 'Well, maybe a wee draw would be nice.'

'The guy turned and looked at him and said, 'Naw – we're gonnae win this.' That was the attitude the supporters had because they had got to the stage where they expected that if we just kept going we would get a victory no matter what the circumstances were. And we could feel that from the crowd, so we were spurred on to that extra effort and more often than not it worked for us.

'Even when we got to the point where we were close to winning the title and maybe the Cup as well, I was never worried about us falling at the final hurdle or anything like that. We had such self-belief that I don't think it occurred to us that we might not do it. We had no reason to have fear.'

Nevertheless, cup semi-finals are notorious for falling flat precisely because although a trophy cannot be won at this stage, it certainly can be lost. For most of the first 45 minutes at Hampden both sides were indecisive, more aware of the chance of making mistakes than the possibility of creating real goalmouth opportunities.

Hearts began with a typical quick flurry upfield and in the first minute Bonner had to sprint to clutch a header from Mike Galloway after John Colquhoun flighted a good cross into the box and the Celtic goalkeeper was called upon again to come for another cross, this time supplied by Kenny Black on the left.

That aside, there was not much constructive football on offer and most of the attacks which made it as far as the penalty areas frittered out before they were likely to inflict damage. McStay was the exception to the general rule of play, coaxing and cajoling from his beat in the centre of the park, willing to seek and win the ball and spreading measured passes towards his forwards.

Celtic's difficulty was that Hearts had put Galloway and Black along with their captain Gary Mackay into the area around him so that apart from McStay's contributions, Celtic's distribution from midfield was being stifled. Mackay's efforts took more out of him than anybody outside the Hearts dressing-room could have guessed because he was suffering from a virus and had to be substituted.

By that time, however, Hearts had taken the lead. The goal arrived on the hour mark and in keeping with the shape of the contest up to then, it was a scrappy piece of work. Brian Whittaker pushed upfield from left back and saw that Dave McPherson was making ground towards the Celtic box. Whittaker lobbed a hopeful cross ahead of his team-mate but there was nothing to suggest that Celtic were in any danger from the move until Bonner and McPherson contested the ball in the air.

Some Celtic players were already claiming that McPherson had been offside when Whittaker released the ball. They had much more to protest about within another second or so because not only did McPherson appear to push Bonner, but the ball also dropped over the pair and into the empty net. Whittaker could not have imagined such an outcome when he hoisted the ball optimistically into the area but the referee, Kenny Hope, signalled the goal and the Hearts full back found his name on the scoresheet for the first time that season, to the equal astonishment of McStay.

'It was a blow, all right. I didn't feel we had been playing all that well but I thought we were getting there and I certainly didn't feel we were in any danger when Brian Whittaker put the ball in. It was a strange goal and coming quite late in a semi-final it was a real boost for Hearts. But sometimes during the '88 season it seemed that we might need that sort of thing to happen to us to make us shift up a gear. That's the effect the Hearts goal had on us and I felt after they had scored it that they wouldn't get another one in the game but that if we just kept going and didn't panic we would probaly score at least one.'

Hearts had got what they came for and now their strategy was to hold their advantage for the half hour which remained. Inevitably they began to retreat by degrees towards their own goal and McStay now found increasing space in which to direct operations. At one point it seemed that he had found the elusive opening as he held off a challenge inside the area and released Frank McAvennie with a breathtaking pass but the striker was undermined by anxiety and he struck his attempt wide of the target from eight yards.

Celtic's chances began to multiply. McAvennie had the goal in sight again when he went up for a header at the sort of range which was usually a formality for him. This time he put his effort over the crossbar. There was a momentary groan of frustration from the massed Celtic support behind Henry Smith's goal but soon the familiar pulse of roared encouragement resumed its beat. Mark McGhee replaced Joe Miller and worked his way into a good position a few yards out only to find a cross from Chris Morris sweep across the goalmouth just out of reach of Andy Walker and himself.

Celtic were beating Hearts like a gong yet still the decisive touch in front of goal would not materialise. Nobody on the field could have been in any doubt about how little life was left in the contest because with ten minutes remaining the first fretful Hearts fans had begun to whistle for Kenny Hope to stop the proceedings and by the time his watch showed three minutes of normal time still to run, the cacophony from the maroon ranks was ear-splitting. McStay remained unperturbed.

'It still didn't go through my mind that we would lose. As long as there was time we would keep playing, we all knew that, and Hearts knew it, too. The voice in my head was saying, 'Keep going, keep going – you'll get this goal.' I maybe did think when it was 1–0 that I would settle for one goal and go to a replay but not once we actually scored.

'The goal was a case of dropsy, wasn't it? Maybe you better not put that in case big Henry decides to kill me, but we got a corner kick and when Tommy Burns put it over I thought Henry was going to get it. It didn't work out that way. The ball dropped for

Roy Aitken and he cut it in for Mark McGhee and he swung round
and stuck it away through a lot of bodies.

'I thought it was a lot to do with the amount of pressure we had
put them under for such a long spell. You need a wee break in that
situation but the longer you've got them under pressure the more
likely you are to get it and that's the way it worked out. Then once
the goal goes in you have all your self-confidence again and you're
saying to yourself that it doesn't matter whether there's 30 seconds
or 30 minutes left in the game, let's go and get this win.'

The match edged into injury time and by now apprehension had
silenced the Hearts contingent as Celtic kept battering at Smith's
goal. The Tynecastle side had lost one avoidable goal. With their
confidence rapidly fraying they were about to concede another, just
as soft. Once more the goal came from a high ball, this time a cross
by Billy Stark on the right, and once more Smith should have cut
it out but the goalkeeper allowed McGhee to come across him for a
header which would probably have gone in under its own power;
Andy Walker stabbed it over the line to make sure.

The Hearts players were utterly stricken, none more so than
Smith, as the wall of noise from the cavorting Celtic fans behind
their goal swept over them. There was no time left for them to
make even a token attempt to save the game and nobody in the
crowd of 65,886 thought that the final whistle was anything other
than a mercy for them.

'I can look back now and say I've been in the same situation as
the Hearts lads and I know how much it hurts when you've been
gutted like that. I've been through that, too. If you're strong you
get over it. But I wasn't feeling sorry for Hearts at the end of the
game because I felt that we worked exceptionally hard that
afternoon and I thought the least we deserved was a draw.

'If we'd had to settle for a draw I would have taken it but I would
have been disappointed. I felt we were worth a win for all our
efforts and I'll settle for a winning goal in injury time every time.
I thought it was a wonderful game, not just because we won it as
we did but because of the way we played once we got going. It was
about the way we are as a club when we're at our best.

'We never gave in. We always believed we would win and the
supporters felt exactly the same way. It was one of those
afternoons when the crowd and the players were tuned in to each
other. It wasn't just that we knew it was our game, it was our year.
Big Roy Aitken sticks in my mind because just before we scored the

second goal he was shouting, "Come on! Come on! We're going to win this." Well, you're not going to argue with him are you? When you've somebody like that behind you it all turns into sheer belief that you will win it.'

Hearts did achieve a modicum of revenge on the following Saturday at Tynecastle when they beat Celtic 2–1 to postpone the inevitable annexation of the title, not that the Parkhead directors can have been unduly depressed because the result meant a vast home gate of 70,000 a week later when Dundee were beaten 3–0 on 23 April.

The flag flew again over Celtic Park, the support had demonstrated the huge resources available to the club when all within it were working in harmony and, as Tommy Burns recounts elsewhere, there was still the bonus delight of a thrilling Scottish Cup final against Dundee United which would complete Celtic's 11th double in one hundred years of eventful existence. Like Burns, though, McStay believes an immense opportunity to compete with Rangers was squandered.

'It should have been a springboard to better things but I think we've all learned that either there wasn't the money there or maybe the directors just thought they could get away with saving the pennies and believed they had a strong enough squad to go and win a few more championships.

'The next year it was the Scottish Cup we won but the signs were that the squad was ageing and that we would need replacements. After that Cup win in 1989 the experienced players more or less disappeared and then apart from Packie in goal it was myself and Peter Grant who were left to hold the fort outfield. Peter was 23 and I was 25. It was a lot to handle, to be truthful.

'The captaincy was given to me which was a great honour but I suppose I look back and feel hurt, mainly for the fans, that what should have taken us on to more success simply didn't happen. Thankfully that is all in the past and you've seen what goes on here. Under Tommy Burns we've had a season with only one league defeat and we've been buying better players to strengthen the team. We're investing and improving and although the improvement hasn't yet been met with all the success we would want, we're getting there. But it should have been done back in '88.

'There were many hard times before it was realised what was needed at this club. At the start of every season you have such hope for what lies ahead and each year began like that for myself and the fans. Sometimes we even got off to a good start but it was the staying power and professionalism you need when the going gets rough which was missing.

'The difference between Celtic when I first came here or when I was in the centenary team was that we had players who knew what the club was all about and who could find that extra percentage to dig us out of a difficult patch. Every club has these patches even if they're successful but when we had our bad spells they simply seemed to go on and on. By the time we picked up again everything was lost. There were a few seasons like that.

'The longer those bad spells went on, the trophyless years, the more the relationship between the crowd and the players changed. Instead of all of us believing we would win even when games were going against us, there would be a fair amount of nervousness around. If somebody maybe didn't get a pass or a shot right early in the game the crowd would be anxious and we would feel that. It went back and forward like that and it got worse. That, aligned with what was going on behind the scenes, the takeover attempts and the trouble in the boardroom, made it a very unsettling place.

'We could feel the fans getting frustrated and quite rightly so because they had other worries beside the games. They were concerned about the way the club was going but they couldn't release that frustration and unhappiness anywhere else but at games. At that period, coming up towards the takeover, this was a bad place to come and work. Some mornings I would wake up and think, oh, no – what kind of day is this going to be?

'You knew it was such an unsettling atmosphere. Compare it with Celtic Park now. I love the place. This is the way it should always be, happy and lively. I did have a wee worry about my contract two years ago. I could see everything changing for the better and I wanted to be part of it, to play in what was going to be a magnificent ground. But the gaffer had left me out of the team and I didn't know what was happening because he was building a squad and chopping and changing things.

'So when I was left out I found it difficult. Maybe I was going to be surplus, or whatever. I looked out at this ground after the Scottish Cup final we won and said to myself, I just want to play in front of this. I just want to be here when it's all finished, especially after coming through so many hard years. It worked out well, though – I think the gaffer was just noising me up, really.

'To go back to the time before that when I thought that maybe I might leave the club about four years ago, I said at the time the only place which would have taken me away from here was the move to Italy that was talked about. I had set my sights on it but my attitude was, if it happens, great. If not, I didn't want to shut the door on Celtic. A lot of people were pressurising me to say whether I was going or staying, even at the turn of the year when I still had five months of my contract left.

'So it was a hard situation to handle and I tried to keep it quiet as much as I could but in the latter stages I just got fed up with it all. Even when I threw my jersey into the Jungle it was because if I had decided to go I would have regretted not doing that and saying thank you to the fans. I had heard players before saying they were sorry they never had a chance to say goodbye.

'But then when the contract offer came up in 1992 I had to refuse it because that's just the way the process works. They send you a contract, you refuse it if you want to keep your options open. Once the press got a whiff of that it was a case of 'Paul McStay's going'. I remember an interview with one reporter where I explained to him that to refuse a new contract sometimes was just part of the procedure.

'He said to me, "Aye, but you are going, aren't you?" It was this pressure to commit myself. Yet I knew and I spoke to Liam Brady about it, that there were offers coming in from England and being politely turned down. Everton were one club. I spoke to Mr Kendall. Blackburn were interested and I spoke to Mr Dalglish . . . the top man. I spoke to Mr Souness as well. He was very keen but a couple of weeks later he said, no, it wasn't to be, he was looking at someone else.

'Those were the ones I spoke to but there were other clubs interested, acting through agents. As I say, though, I had set my sights on Italy and maybe I was stubborn, but when I looked at all the offers I thought that the only place that could possibly take me away from Celtic Park would have to be somewhere special. It didn't materialise and I was very pleased that Celtic kept the door open for me, that they wanted me to stay, because I would never have shut the door on Celtic.

'Playing for a club like this that you've supported and been brought up from an early age to love, and being allowed to do something about that out on the park – and being captain – is something that every single Celtic fan wants to do. That kept me going through the bad spells. It made me try harder and some people thought maybe I was trying too hard, running myself into the ground. Look at Peter Grant as well, Charlie Nicholas, the others who came up through the system, they understand what it's all about at Celtic. They know what it takes and the fans love them for that.

'The first thing we all want for Celtic is success. We got that in the 1995 Scottish Cup final when we beat Airdrie. We needed to lift that trophy and we did it, so I'll always say that was a great game. But we all hope for a special performance and speaking personally, I'll always remember the Hearts game in '88 for that reason. It's up there for me along with the '88 final against Dundee United and winning the league against St Mirren on the last day of the '86 season.

'I had happy times here once before. Now I've been part of better times again, part of the revolution which has happened here. I thought that I might not be here for all this but I am, and I'm very, very grateful . . . '

Paul McStay was forced to retire at the end of the 1996–97 season when doctors advised him that a persistent ankle injury meant that he had to stop playing.

Jim Craig

REAL MADRID 0 CELTIC 1

7 June 1967

IN sport there is only one thing more to be done once you have proved you are the best.

Prove it again.

Celtic's opportunity to demonstrate that they were absolute monarchs of all they could survey in Europe came only 13 days after their astounding triumph in Lisbon, when they took the field in the San Bernabeu stadium to play Real Madrid in a benefit game for the Spanish side's legendary maestro, Alfredo di Stefano, the Argentinian footballer who can be regarded without contradiction – even in an activity where exaggeration is almost an occupational obligation – as one of the sport's greatest practitioners.

That Celtic should have been invited to grace this occasion was the most eloquent testimony to Jock Stein's insistence on directing his players' endeavours towards expanding the game's creative possibilities. To emphasise their admiration for the Scots, representatives of di Stefano's testimonial committee had asked Celtic to play in the San Bernabeu before the outcome of the European Cup final was known. Their foresight was massively endorsed when a capacity crowd of 130,000 – the Spanish press had forecast 70,000 – turned out to witness the meeting of European football's legendary masters and their latest successors.

There were some connected with Celtic who wondered whether Stein was asking his team to play one game too many after what had been an unsurpassable season, one which had begun on 13 August with a 2–0 victory over Hearts at Tynecastle in the League Cup, the first of a clean sweep of domestic trophies which would be annexed over the next nine months before the golden evening in

Lisbon. In addition, there had been the burden of international demands on the likes of Ronnie Simpson, Tommy Gemmell, Willie Wallace and Bobby Lennox, all of whom had taken part in Scotland's remarkable demolition of England when the world champions were played off their own Wembley turf in April.

Some of the Lisbon detachments had not yet returned from Portugal, having adapted the return journey into a glorious bodega-bistro-pub crawl home. Amongst those who had made it back or who had not been able to witness events on the banks of the Tagus except by television, there were hangovers which would be topped up right through the Glasgow Fair fortnight.

So, went the argument amongst the more timid, would it not be better to let the celebrations proceed unchecked by the possibility of an anti-climax in Spain? Stein's blunt retort was that after the excessive demands of an unparalleled season the players had earned the right to parade their skills in an exhibition game before they dispersed to their holiday destinations. Not that Stein had the slightest intention of permitting them to treat di Stefano's benefit show as anything other than an opportunity to confirm their status as the supreme football power in Europe. Stein had another answer to the question of what to do once his team had proved they were the best.

Prove they were even better.

For di Stefano, the game would be a valedictory salute from a team which had revolved around his role as a deep-lying centre forward on the field and a temperamental autocrat off it. His medal collection was awesome and contained souvenirs of one World Club championship, five European Cup successes and eight Spanish championships. He had been voted European footballer of the year twice. He had scored a staggering 49 goals for Real Madrid in the European Cup between 1955–56 and 1963–64, including three in the legendary final of 1960 when Eintracht Frankfurt were thrashed 7–3 at Hampden Park.

In the first 11 years of the European Cup's existence only four clubs had seen their names engraved on the trophy and all were from Latin countries. Real Madrid were six times winners, Benfica and Inter took it twice each and AC Milan made up the total before Celtic emerged unexpectedly from the pale north. It was as though Celtic had been summoned to have their examination result cross-checked. Stein understood this very well and instructed his travelling squad that they must take the game entirely seriously.

It would be a contrast in styles, not merely a comparison of the cream of British football with the elite of the Spanish game, but also a collision between Latin and northern temperaments.

For Jim Craig, life had already presented itself as a remarkable set of contrasts. Having combined a career as Celtic's right back with the discipline required to achieve a degree in dentistry, he obviously had to be excepted from the widespread belief that when a footballer visited a chiropodist it was to request brain surgery. In punning recognition of his name and diverse talents, his team-mates nicknamed him Cairney (after the actor John Cairney, who played a schoolteacher in the '60s TV drama series *This Man Craig*). Jim Craig's mind and feet were educated in Govan but his football horizons were expanded by his father at an early age.

'I went to St Anthony's primary school and St Gerard's secondary school where, of course, they were all Celtic fans but in addition to that my father was a Leithite who had come through in his mid-20s to live in Glasgow. Dad obviously had a great penchant for Hibs as well, so my boyhood heroes were the Celtic team of the day plus the Famous Five – Smith, Johnstone, Reilly, Turnbull and Ormond – who played football the way I like to see football played, with a wee bit of dash and spice and vigour.

'I started playing for the primary school, the big skinny guy at the back. It was one of the problems of my career that I kept asking to play up front and no teacher would let me because I was always the type of boy they put at centre half and on the odd occasion when I did get a shot in attack I was no sooner there than they would lose a goal and I was moved back again. So I played all through St Gerard's and then I played for Scottish Schools two years running, in my fifth year and sixth year, and I captained the team in my second season.

'Actually, I played along with Andy Roxburgh both years. We lost to England the first year when we went down to play in Burnley and trained in Preston and I had the great privilege of meeting Tom Finney who, of course, was a much greater name 35 years ago than he is now. At that time there were a few clubs speaking to my father about my signing for them but I was quite keen to go on to university and I knew a lot of guys dropped out after a year because they found it hard going so I thought I wouldn't play very much in my first year and just get my head down.

'In fact, I played for the Celtic third team intermittently, having signed for them on amateur forms. And then second year chemistry was extremely tough because you're doing anatomy, physiology and biochemistry and you're on a nine-to-six shift with Saturday morning work as well. Plus, your studying has to come after that so there was really no time for anything else. In second year and part of third year I didn't play senior football at all.

'If I had a wee bit of time I would take my boots over to Bellahouston Park and get a game for any team that was a man short. I played for quite a variety of teams, like Weir's Recreation, RanCel – which was the combined Rangers and Celtic supporters' team – and a fair number of others. It was a case of Have Boots, Will Travel.

'Celtic were very understanding, fortunately for me. Sean Fallon was very good at looking out for me as was a scout for whom I have a lot to thank, Joe Connors, who's now dead. Joe was always turning up at those Saturday afternoon games and unknown to me he was keeping Sean in touch with the situation. In my fourth year I started playing for the University. I played from the start of the season in August 1964 I was playing regularly and I got a Scottish cap in October. About early December Sean came to see me and asked if I would be interested in signing for Celtic.

'I was really taken aback because I had got away from that scene to a certain extent. I was still following it because my dad was a great sports fan and there was a lot of chat at home about football but I hadn't been watching any. I went to see the Dean at the Dental Hospital and asked him what he thought. He was very good and said that since I was four-and-a-half years through my course the chances of me dropping out were not very high, so I could go ahead.

'I actually remember asking him, "What happens if the worst comes to the worst and I make the first team?" And he said they would be flexible because they would be quite happy to have a lad with a side like Celtic. So I signed in January of 1965 which was two months before Jock came. I was signed by Sean and Jimmy McGrory. Mr McGrory took me in to meet the board – and this is true as I'm sitting here telling you – I was introduced to Bob Kelly, who offered me the back of his left hand to shake. He had a withered hand because of an accident as a child but I didn't know that.

'I was completely flummoxed because nobody had ever done that to me before and I remember taking it in both hands to be on the safe side. Then I was introduced to Desmond White who was the club secretary. And he had walked into a propellor with his right arm during the war and he handed out the back of his left hand as well. I was totally confused but I took his hand in both my hands as well.

'I was beginning to think that this must be a club custom. Maybe you had to lose an arm to get a directorship but then Tom Devlin was the third one and he burst out laughing because he obviously saw my predicament. He said, "I'm the normal one" and after that it was fine.

'I played the rest of that season in the reserves and made the first team in October of that year in a European tie at home (*this was a Cup Winners Cup tie on 7 October against Go-Ahead Eagles of Holland who were trailing 6–0 from the first leg; Celtic won the second leg 1–0*) and then another home tie against Aarhus and after that I started playing regularly for the first team from then on.

'After spending four years paying for the dentistry final year dinner I was playing in Kiev when it took place and I was ordered off into the bargain. At the dinner the Dean said, "There are two Craigs in this class. There's John Craig and there's the other fella who disgraced himself in Russia tonight."

'When I came back one of the surgeons said, "Did you hear what the Dean said about you?" I said, "No, tell me." The surgeon said, "He said you were a disgrace."

'In fact, I was a victim of circumstances when I was ordered off. The winger and myself had been needling but then somebody punched me. Next thing I knew the winger and myself were both sent off. So this surgeon said, "Right, go and tell him that. Don't stand for any nonsense."

'I went in and said, "You apparently said something at the dinner which was untrue." And he said, "So I understand and I'd like to extend my apologies to you." I went to my class and we were in the middle of a lecture when the Dean stuck his head round the door and said, "I'd just like to say I was very sharp with Mr Craig and I was wrong."

'I thought, "What a big man. He didn't need to do that." But I filed it away in my head for future reference because there are times when you are wrong and you may as well come out and say so. If more people did that the world might be a better place.'

Certainly, Craig's world was rapidly improving. He graduated as a dentist and increasingly established himself as a regular in the

Celtic side, although he had competition from Willie O'Neill, a steady and consistent full back whom Stein also liked. Craig, though, had one advantage which ultimately told; he had been an active athlete at school and his pace and stamina were to be crucial in his role as a fast overlapping full back in an attacking team.

'Before Jock came we didn't train with a ball. The lads like myself who were training at night were very fit, mind you. At nights there were guys like Jim Brogan, Gerry Sweeney, Tony Taylor, who went on to play for Crystal Palace, and wee John Gorman, who's now Glenn Hoddle's assistant with England. Graeme Souness was there and I used to run him to the station and give him stick for being too fat.

'The team which Jock inherited wasn't too much different from the side which won the European Cup. I would think that when you come into a place the first team that does it for you would be the one you'd regard as a wee bit special. The team which won the Scottish Cup against Dunfermline was that for Jock. Ian Young was at full back in the place I would later fill, Yogi Hughes was there and Charlie Gallagher and Bertie Auld were fighting for places, so not a lot of difference, really.

'I think where it landed lucky for me was that I was always getting stick at school for coming forward and in those days full backs and centre halves were generally expected to stay in their own half. I went to a coaching course at St Augustine's which wasn't under SFA auspices. It was run by a private individual who was all for me at full back just pushing the ball to my wing half. As a 15-year-old you don't like to usurp authority but I had a word with this man one evening and said, "My problem is this guy in front of me can't play. I've given him the ball and he can't do the things I can do, so why can't I take it up the field and he stays back?"

'The answer was, "No, the way to do is that the full back gives it to the wing half and that's it." Now I'm talking about the time around 1958 when the Brazilians had started to play 4–2–4 and I was fighting my corner just about the period when teams were beginning to adapt their systems.

'When Jock came it was liberating for me because he revolutionised the way we played. At training the bibs played the non-bibs, the same teams every morning. If two of your guys were injured, say, it didn't matter. You had to play without them and it was really competitive. If Jock happened to be playing for one side or the other it could go on forever until he got the right result.

'It meant that everything was done on a very competitive level whereas if you're only doing lapping, you're only really doing it for yourself. The night-time lads who had been training together were all fit and most of them were pretty fast but as soon as there were groups split against each other, with the winning group getting away early then you start fighting for each other and cajoling your team-mates. I think football training should be like that and I sometimes wonder if the European players who come to this country to play understand that. We have to compete. We don't have enough skill not to.

'Having said that, of course, the team that Jock took to the European Cup final did have the skill. The chances of a Scottish team ever winning the European Cup again with only Scottish players is slim, to say the least. It was really a freak of circumstances and what made it even more of a freak was that apart from the odd incomer the team was there waiting to be resurrected, which just shows how someone can simply walk in and see what was latent and waiting to bloom.

'Bertie, Charlie and Bobby Murdoch were good passers of the ball. Gemmell and myself were extremely fit and comfortable on the ball for full backs, because don't forget that in the mid '60s most fullbacks were of the traditional variety. With Rangers, for example, Bobby Shearer and then Davie Provan didn't come forward too much whereas Tommy and myself would get into the opposition box and take guys on and it was no big problem for Jock.

'Also, although we had a smallish goalkeeper in Ronnie Simpson, Gemmell, myself and Billy were all six-footers and in our own way we were all centre halfs, so there was rarely a problem with the high ball coming in. Up front we had runners and we had wee Jimmy, who was maybe not always as effective over the period as he might have been but who was absolutely wonderful at upsetting a defence. And when Whispy (*Willie Wallace*) came and poor Joe McBride got injured, once again our strength was straight through the middle.

'I believe that was what was missing from Celtic when we had that wonderful league run in '95–'96, playing very attractive football but scoring less than two goals a game. Our team knew how to head in the direction of goal.

'Speaking of direction, incidentally, brings to mind one aspect of the European Cup final which I can never forget because it surprised me so much. We had the only bus driver in the whole of Portugal who didn't know the way to the National Stadium. You know how it is when you're sitting on the bus for any length of time before a big game and it can be bit nerve wracking. We used to feel the nerves coming up from Seamill to Hampden to meet the police escort at Barrhead.

'Well, this guy was going in the wrong direction and suddenly all the players started shouting, "Hey, boss, why is everybody else going the other way?" So we arrived quite late at the ground and I have always believed that the driver taking the wrong road actually helped us because the nerves were gone by the time we got there.

'And then underneath the stadium – you've got to picture this – Ronnie looked an old man in '67, even older without his teeth, Bertie walked like a cripple and wee Jimmy was a midget. We came out into this tunnel and these Italians were standing there wearing a beautiful vertical blue and black strip, cutaway boots, oiled thighs gleaming in the sun and all that.

'Then this group of odd allsorts came out opposite them and wee Jimmy is shouting to Facchetti – and this is perfectly true – he's shouting, "Haw, big man, efter the gemme, swap the jerseys." And Facchetti's looking at us and saying, "What the . . . ?"

'If any neutral had seen us they would have said we had no right to win, but we did win and I'm eternally grateful to have had the opportunity to be part of all of that. It's odd how memory works. I have two particular recollections of the game. One is that my father had not wanted to come because he thought we were going to lose and he did not wish to come all that way to see us beaten.

'But I had said to him, "You've got to come. I've got you a ticket." So the Saturday beforehand he'd decided to come and he enlisted a pal from Bishopbriggs and the pair of them headed out to Lisbon on a three-day package. People still ask me all the time, "What were you thinking after you brought down Cappellini and gave away the penalty kick?"

'I couldn't get it out of my head that I could imagine what my dad was thinking up there. In the midst of all this mayhem some players were saying, "Aw, Cairney, for Christ's sake!" and others were saying there was an injustice. I think myself that, having been told that Cappellini was good at cutting the ball back, I wanted to make sure that if he did he would bang into me and when he did I knocked him over. I don't think I deliberately set out to foul him. But while all that was going on I could imagine my father saying, "Aye, I told you, didn't I?"

'The second memory is that at the end of the game I met my uncle Philip and he was crying. He was a bachelor and my godfather and he'd been to the Olympic Games in 1936 and travelled all over Europe since then, but that evening he was sitting crying because it was the greatest day of his life. He was 57 years old and I found it funny to see an adult crying like that because of a football match. I've seen it a good few times since then, mind you, but at that time it struck me as quite something to see a staid and sensible man in tears about a game.

'I think there were people in tears when we took the Cup round Celtic Park on the Friday night but from a personal point of view I was struck by what the French call the *coup de foudre*. Although James Farrell, who was to become my father-in-law, was a Celtic director, his daughter Elizabeth never attended football matches. I had met her casually before once at a function but I did have a connection with her which was quite an ice-breaker.

'When you sit your finals you do a filling as part of the exam and I didn't have a suitable cavity to fill. What they do in a case like this is they bring in a few patients with something suitable and you're handed a set of X-rays and invited to choose one. And as it happened, it was Liz's younger sister. So on the Friday night at Celtic Park I saw Liz and was smitten, which makes that particular evening very memorable to me for reasons not connected with football.

'Anyway, that weekend was given over to celebration and we went back to Celtic Park on the Tuesday. When we got back inside Jock said, "We're going to see this game." There was a general reaction of, "Boss, we won it. What are we wanting to watch it again for?" Jock was quite annoyed about this and he said no, we should always watch our triumphs and pick out the bits we didn't do properly and wouldn't want to repeat.

'So we did watch it. As we went through it he didn't pick out the more obvious points. It was more a case of, "See that there – if you had maybe gone wide a wee bit earlier we could maybe have got in behind them." It was all those comments, the sort of things which are very easy to see on a film. Then he announced that we had

181

been made an offer to play one more game and that we had accepted it.

'I assumed it was some sort of charity game and that we would be playing Berwick Rangers for the good of the Borders or whatever. The next thing he said was that di Stefano was going to have a benefit and that we'd been asked to be the team to play Real Madrid. There was a kind of stunned silence. Somebody said, "Boss, you're kidding?" He said, "No, we're going." There were a few who thought, great, we're going to get a few nights in Madrid, but the more perceptive ones, including myself, tended to say, "Boss, we've just won the European Cup. Why are we putting it on the line?"

'His answer was, "Aye, well if you're good enough you'll go over there and beat them."

'They had just won the Spanish championship so there was a wee bit of reaction which Jock quickly stamped on and we had to get ourselves back into training again. Once we got into the way of it the talk was all about who we might be going to play against. There would be di Stefano obviously and for me that was a very impressive prospect.

'I had been an 18-year-old schoolboy in the Schoolboys' Enclosure at Hampden Park for the European Cup final in 1960. I read a book which mentioned this final and it said that Real were the team everybody in the crowd wanted to win that night. I think that is totally wrong because the crowd contained a lot of Celtic supporters who wanted bloody Eintracht Frankfurt to win on the grounds that any team which could beat Rangers 12–4 would do as far as they were concerned. The greatest tribute you could pay Real Madrid was that they won everybody round by imposing their style on the game even after the Germans went ahead.

'So all week at training we were animated about who would be up against us. Then it was out to Madrid, nice hotel, all the rest of it, including training at the San Bernabeu. The San Bernabeu is one of those stadia which seems to be almost sheer at the sides and a guy sitting in the top row seems to be able to spit on your head if you're standing on the touchline. I loved grounds which are right on top of you and as soon as I saw it I wanted to play there.

'We were all excited because our reputation was right on the line. We were the team who had come from nowhere and we were playing attractive football. Real Madrid were the team who had been legends for years for playing attractive football and who had been orchestrated by a man who had won seven caps for Argentina and 31 for Spain. Much to my delight I was to play directly against Gento, whom I had seen in the final at Hampden and whom I had admired for many years.

'By the time I played against him I believe his real, sharp pace had gone. He was still quick but I was quicker than he was, although at the height of his powers it might have been a different matter, I'm sure. Maybe the thought of being compared with these guys added a dimension to our play or maybe it was because our confidence had grown a little bit more by beating Inter Milan or perhaps it was just the sheer thrill of being champions of Europe – which was still sinking in – but on the night, Celtic were truly magnificent.

'Every player rose to the occasion. You have got to say that. Every single man was saying to himself, "We won the European Cup and now we'll show them why." Actually, the team that night had a couple of changes from Lisbon. John Fallon took over from Ronnie in goal and Willie O'Neill was in for Steve Chalmers. We came out, the teams lined up and your man came out and was introduced to both sets of players.

'As we all know, a floodlit occasion gives you a great sense of theatre and there was a spotlight beaming down on di Stefano just to add to the whole occasion. Again, in those days strips were not the glamorous items they are now but I had always thought Real Madrid's all-white was something rather special. The number nine jersey was, of course, reserved for di Stefano himself and he played for 14 minutes during which time, to Willie O'Neill's disgust, the great man nutmegged him.

'At the end of his 14 minutes somebody passed to di Stefano and he bent down, picked the ball up, put it under his arm and held his hand in the air. And that was the end of the game for him. Everybody in the San Bernabeu rose. The players rose, too. I clapped him all the way off the park and we saw him eventually away up there on the presidential podium with a spotlight on him, amongst the dignitaries.

'So the game went on and what a game it was, end to end football, brilliantly skilful and very fast. I had my hands full with Gento because he was still a very good player. There were individual contests, man to man, all over the park. Then suddenly wee Jimmy began to turn it on and the whole stadium responded to him. He was playing in that almost obsessive way he sometimes had, where you thought he wouldn't be content until he'd had a dribble round their entire team. It was an unforgettable display and I'll guarantee there are people in Madrid who tell their grandchildren about how he performed that night.'

The match was a compelling display of attacking football by two sides of vast ability. The *Glasgow Herald* reported it in the dry, abbreviated style it used to employ, but even then the catalogue of incident conveys something of the matchless fare produced by both teams: 'Real played six forwards and never allowed Celtic to establish the midfield domination they established against Inter Milan.

'Real's outside left, Amancio, struck a shot off the falling body of Fallon. In the 31st minute Wallace, Lennox and Gemmell combined but Junquera pushed the ball around the post with a fine leap. After 37 minutes Velasquez hit the bar with a shot from 40 yards.

'With 69 minutes played Real were applying heavy pressure but Celtic got the ball to Johnstone who dribbled 40 yards past three startled defenders (*to this day wee Jimmy insists he beat five of them*) and slipped the ball to Lennox, who shot low and hard under Junquera's falling body.

'It was a classic example of quick modern counter-attack, perfectly executed, aimed at catching the opposition on the wrong foot'.

The *Daily Record* reported: 'Both teams were going all out and the pace was furious. Celtic should have gone ahead when a brilliant pass by Johnstone found Craig but a defender came to Real's rescue.'

The late Hugh Taylor, the *Record*'s perceptive football writer declared: 'The first half was one of the most thrilling I have ever seen, greatly appreciated by the huge Spanish crowd and certainly much better than the European Cup final.'

Lennox's goal, manufactured fittingly by Johnstone's audacity, lifted the closing 20 minutes into overdrive. Stung by the prospect of defeat, not only in front of their own supporters but in the presence of the legend they had come to honour, Real begun to hurl themselves at Celtic. Now, too, was the time for Stein's players to display their deep-rooted pride allied to skills of an order which mesmerised the colossal multitude of spectators on the swooping slopes of the San Bernabeu.

With 15 minutes left, the quickened blood on both sides sparked an incident which reduced the complement of players who would finish the game. Amancio and Auld were sent off for what the *Herald* termed 'an outbreak of fist fighting.' Hugh Taylor's enjoyment of the proceeding's extended to the pugilism, which he described as 'one of the most stirring punchups of the season'.

Meanwhile, at least one unfortunate Real defender found himself the victim of a technical knockout administered by Johnstone and watched in some awe by Jim Craig.

'Jimmy was running riot, so much so that a few minutes from the end their full back, de Felipe, turned his back on him. Now if you were playing for Real Madrid you were up to Spanish international standard but this guy just chucked it because Jimmy had beaten him every way you can possibly beat a full back – inside his legs, outside him, through him, round him and back again. And eventually de Felipe just held up his hands and in any language what he was saying was "Aw naw! Enough!"

'So at the end our whole team was utterly delighted because we've not only won the European Cup, we've shown we can beat any team you care to name.'

Real Madrid may have been losers in front of their own people but both the crowd and their players were sporting about the manner of their defeat. Jimmy Johnstone was startled to be embraced and kissed by Ferenc Puskas, whose status was almost as godlike as that of di Stefano.

Jock Stein told the assembled press: 'I was tremendously proud of our lads for continuing to carry the flag for Celtic and Scotland. We played magnificently against a side determined to beat us. Puskas, Santamaria and di Stefano were all full of praise for Celtic's pace, skill and professional approach to the game.'

For Celtic and their hosts the festivities did not stop with the final whistle. Craig found part of the aftermath literally dazzling.

'They treated us to a reception at which I have never seen so many trophies. You looked at them, you rubbed your eyes and you looked again. Imagine a ballroom with one wall covered by di Stefano's trophies from everywhere. I mean, I read just some of them and they were from football people all over the world. One was a gold ball – "Presented by the Saudi Arabia Football Association to Alfredo di Stefano" – hundreds of trophies and shields and medals, and I mean hundreds, all with inscriptions like that.

'And the fun hadn't finished yet because the next morning I was coming down for breakfast in our hotel and as I passed Jimmy

Johnstone's room he and his wife Agnes were just coming out. She had come over for the game because they were going to go on holiday immediately after it.

'I said to Jimmy, "Where are you off to, wee man?" He said, "We're away our holidays from here." I said, "Oh, I didn't realise that." So I helped him down with the cases and he went back and brought Agnes down and we stood at the front door of the hotel chatting away about the game and so on. The porter hails a cab for Jimmy and I take the cases down and stow them in the boot and I say, "All the best, the two of you, have a good holiday and see you when you get back."

'Jimmy says, "Aye, thanks, same to yourself." And then I hear him saying to the driver, "Benidorm", just as the guy's putting the car into gear.

'The driver looks at him and says "Que?" Jimmy says, "Benidorm".

'The driver says "Que?" again but this time his voice is getting squeaky.

'Jimmy looks up as if he's wondering what the kerfuffle is all about and says, "Benidorm." Now the driver goes into a torrent of Spanish, the upshot of which was, "I'm not going to ****ing Benidorm." But eventually he gave in and took them and it cost Jimmy some ridiculous sum.

'It had been such a wonderful trip and that was the perfect ending. The look on the driver's face was exactly the same as the expression on de Felipe's the night before. I think de Felipe must have been saying "Que?" as well. That's the effect wee Jimmy had on people.

'What will live in my mind forever – apart from the look on that driver's face – was the reception that the Spanish crowd gave us. Crowds aren't daft. They know when they're watching a great game of football. They came to pay tribute to di Stefano and in the end they were rising to Jimmy and saying of Celtic, "This is a right good side."

'We had won the European Cup less than two weeks before and we might have been expected to slip into a trough. Yet we played even better than we had done in Lisbon. We went into the equivalent of the Colosseum and the crowd were saluting us at the finish. All of that is in my memory because I have never seen the di Stefano game again on film and I've seen the highlights of Lisbon only very occasionally.

'I can't afford to live in the past. You'll see I don't have any mementos around. I think there's a tendency to wallow a little bit. Nowadays I have a job to do as a dentist and I try to keep fit and play touch rugby every week throughout the summer. I do collect memorabilia for other people and I'm a great admirer of other folk's talents but one of the problems of being a footballer is that the peaks in your life come at a very early age and I think you have to try and get past that.

'When we have the 30th anniversary of Lisbon it's going to be a bit of a problem for me because I honestly would rather not spend my time involved in all that nostalgia. But if you're asking me I would have to say that the game in Madrid was a greater performance than the game in Lisbon because against Inter we had been underdogs, but against Real we were there to be shot down.

'Instead, we rose to the occasion just as Jock had told us we would do – and that is all you can ask of any team.'

Index